Still Life with BOTTLE

THE OLDEST POT STILL in SCOTLAND (on learning that the HEAVY DUTY imposed on the RESULT of all its hard and steaming WORK goes to the 'BRITISH GOVERNMENT)

Still Life with Bottle

WHISKY ACCORDING TO
RALPH STEADMAN

Harcourt Brace & Company
New York   San Diego   London

Acknowledgements

There are Art Directors and then there are Directors of Art, and then again Art, Directors of. They are all useless and I loathe their meddling in my attempts to fill a vacuum as self-indulgently as is humanly possible. They leech on to the essence of your idea and then claim it as their own. That is what they get paid for. They also get paid for putting as much distance between an author and his creation as is possible, without resorting to physical violence, in order to preserve the sanctity of office life inside a publishing house. They are known to a few of us exclusive authors as book bouncers. However, once in every generation one comes along who is not only a brick but who excels in every aspect of . . . but I digress. My thanks to IAN CRAIG, Art Director of my whole life, who once again has bound me to the mast, blocked my ears against the wail of tempting sirens and steered me clear away from the rocks of my own blind folly.

Editors are in the main loathesome jelly, slimy moss on rocks, accumulated fluff from beneath a restless spirit's mattress, and on occasions the scrapings from a great man's dandruff. But, once in every last decade of a millenium, one wanders in out of the desert and rewrites the Bible or something and expects to get paid for it as well. Operating from a bedsit above a launderette in Lyme Regis and trading under the unlikely handle of LOMAX, Private Investigator, I had hired him to keep an eye on my wife but caught him looking through my papers and trying to cook his head in the microwave. I could tell he had literary aspirations when he asked me if I kept a thick red pencil about me. So I let him loose on my bulky manuscript, the undistilled ramblings of all my investigations into moofling vapours euphaungulating through the mists of time. With commendable ferocity he went through it like a combine harvester in overdrive. However, copies of the full unexpurgated text of my deepest imaginings can be obtained from the above premises in Lyme Regis, or would have been if the fool hadn't trashed the whole lot in the wastebasket of my Scottish Macintosh Performa 400 in a fit of Jacobite pique. Being Scottish himself, he sided with the Macintosh machinery, taking exception to the flippant attitude he believes I have adopted towards a subject that obviously means far more to him than keeping an eye on my wife.

DENISE BATES, or Dennis as she is affectionately known, is in fact a code name for Operation 160, the systematic restriction imposed on all would-be authors who tend to go on a bit and who would waste vast amounts of publishers' money which otherwise can be put to better use whipping up needy book reps into a selling frenzy at conferences in posh hotels. Operation 160, or Editorial Director to give her the second code name she uses, takes the oil out of turmoil and skilfully uses it to lubricate the wheels of creativity. She holds the reins and drives the wayward energy through a narrow gap, miraculously steering it towards a hopeless deadline, urging it ever onward, until the creation, now wheezing like a damp bagpipe, is taken by the scruff of the neck, stamped on, and printed in time for publication.

ANNA, my wife, who as always saves the hours like rare butterflies and lets them fly inside our lives. She gently guides the silly away into the sunlight of their own making, and helps the time-wasters to light up the shadow of their squander. Deeply involved with her own creations, she nevertheless has time to listen as I groan my thoughts out loud through a bullhorn. She helps to give them form more than she could know. Forever patient . . . how *does* she do it?

Special thanks to JOHN HUGHES at Matthew Gloag, MATTHEW GLOAG himself, JIM MCEWAN at Morrison Bowmore, WILLY MCNEILL at Glen Garioch, and the many kind distillers, blenders, coopers, malters and smugglers who must have wondered what the devil I was up to.

Requests for permission to make copies of any part of the work should be mailed to: Permissions Department, Harcourt Brace & Company, 6277 Sea Harbor Drive, Orlando, Florida 32887-6777.

First published in the United Kingdom in 1994 by Ebury Press, Random House, 20 Vauxhall Bridge Road, London SW1V 2SA

Library of Congress Cataloging-in-Publication Data
Steadman, Ralph.
Still life with bottle: whisky according to Ralph Steadman.
p.   cm.
Originally published: London: Ebury Press, 1994.
Includes index.
ISBN 0-15-100310-6 (hc)
1. Whiskey—Scotland. 2. Steadman, Ralph—Contributions in whiskey. I. Title.
TP605.S74   1997
641.2'52'09411—dc21   97-19469

Printed in the United Arab Emirates
First U.S. edition
A B C D E

Contents

INTRODUCTION 7
The Making of Whisky 10

PREWHISKERY *12*

Ever since man learned to fashion a vessel that would not leak, he has sought to learn the secret of the vapours that would turn to intoxicating nectar . . .

WHISKERY *58*

By coracle from Ireland they came . . .

Index *160*

*WILD WILLY GLENGARGLE was shot in
the bag and deflated between the
Cumlorden retreat and the Gay Gordons. It
was a terrible loss to wind throughout
Scotland. It took three visits to Macklo
Cuskie's wee burn bothy to revive the
deflated parts . . . (an obscure old snippet of
an account of obscure origin).*

Ian Fyfe has worked at Glen Garioch distillery since 1956 and treated me to a private performance of some of his old bothy songs in the reception area referred to as The Bothy. He was accompanied only by Glen Garioch's 10, 15 and 21 year-old malts. He never forgets a single word and starts up the moment you are seated with a glass in your hand, as though he has just been wound up and switched on . . .

BOTHY SONG by IAN FYFE

Noo doon in a wee toon in Buchan
Ah practised fur mony's a year
Every man they said socht
For ye now tae yer horse
He's lookin' a wee bittie queer

Noo I noticed his stirk
In the new tatty park
Wi his tail up and lugs hangin doon
Noo he said
Tell the foreman tae get on his bike
An get the best vet in the toon

Ae nicht wi ma gig an ma shetty
I wid dauner an hame afore dark
An ah hid a wee dram maybe een
Maybe twa
An ah saw a man coming through the tatty park

Cried a fine night
An he never took heed
But ah fun oot in the day
A'd been wasting ma wind
On a scarecrow stuck up in a drill.

IAN FYFE SINGING BOTHY BALLADS ON THE UNACCOMPANIED 10, 15, and 21 YEAR OLD!

INTRODUCTION

A tale of desperate longing, thirst, deceit, ingenuity,
violence, plagiarism, common theft, betrayal, over-
indulgence, duty, death and destruction. A litany of bad
behaviour, secrecy, monopolies, mists of despair,
outrage, penury, butchery, lechery, savagery and
bagpipe karaoke. A history of sorts –
an illicit romance . . .

A whisky trail can take you on a hard and
dangerous journey. Aye, it can be a slippery
slope, an uphill climb and a Pandora's Box of
quaint behaviour and weird moments. Going
into training for such a daunting task is more
a trial by abstinence than of reckless indulgence. Single malt whisky is a drink to be
respected, treasured, savoured, and even
kept for half a lifetime, if necessary, to avoid
it being trashed on an oblivious palate. It is
neither a drink to quench a thirst, nor merely
a drink to look at for very long, when the sun
is going down. It fulfills all of these require-
ments and more. It gathers momentum with
every passing year. It fires dreams in the
depths of despair and it gathers stories inside
itself, as rich and dark as an ancient peat bog.

*'tis a dark bottle so that it does not look ugly when
half empty.'*

Only a Celt could have said something so pes-
simistic and yet so saturated in soulful longing for something not yet finished but sadly,
now, only half the friend it was. The apparent
simplicity of the statement masks a deep,
entrenched and tormented philosophy that
life must be hard no matter how good it
appears to be, and if it is really good, then
there is surely pain around the corner. And
he is right of course.

But it is whisky I am writing about here, so
I have no business getting bogged down in
the dribbling self-pity of a Scotsman in his

cups. The problem is – and I can vouch for
this, after much sojourning in the MacHigh-
lands, the MacLowlands, the McGlens, the
Burns and the Lochries – you cannot separate
the one from the other, and maybe that is the
miracle of it all.

This book will probably float about everywhere like the very vapours that moofle off
the bubbling wort in every pot still from here
to Ballindalloch and back to Tennessee, but
never mind, so long as it gives you, along the
way, a taste for the 'Cratur' itself. The spirit,
and the rich diversity of its nature, is the
thing.

I could never pretend to have seen it all,
much less even taste it all, but what modest
amount I have seen *and* some of the things I
have not seen, I will share with you, like the

rude imaginings of Scottish gossip. Even though they did not invent distillation, the Scots invented the poetry that makes whisky what it is.

Yet it was not always so. To separate the deadly union of self-righteous Calvinism from a god-fearing, guilt-ridden and compulsive alcoholic claim to their very own drink, I must first go down the road of my own choosing in search of any clue to the where-abouts of the first process.

In this world, nothing unique is anybody's in particular, it seems to me, and anybody who says otherwise is a usurper and a charlatan, which includes just about everybody who made a fast buck out of a good idea. It seems to depend on who was in the right place, with the right conditions, at the right time and managed to catch their piece of luck in full flood, as it were, and then flew by the seat of his or her pants until the opposition lost interest, fell by the wayside or was even exterminated. And don't dismiss that as the way of all things either. It is merely a Darwinian theory, but it can work in business, too.

The Grain of Truth

A gnarled industry, deeply bitten and scarred in rich folklore. Feastie Tales, dark as peat, rich and warm as copper stills. Steaming wort and fermenting wash, wafting through the ether like fairy-tale demons. Aye! The stuff of a smuggler's secrecy, distilled from native cunning and filtered through time. The wild, warm inner fire of natural strength. The story of whisky is a saga of human nature versus bureaucratic control. The wisdom of old country ways, trial and error, ingenuity, spirit safes, padlocks, wild extremes and perfect balance.

A whisky blender of years' standing develops a nose saturated to bursting and yet a sixth sense evolves and pierces the plethora of aromas like a steel spike nailing every nuance to its mast. It is probably the nearest a human being will ever get to emulating the homing instinct of a salmon, swimming up-river to breed.

What I imagined of whisky distilling, distilleries, regions and traditions and the reality of what I saw, were pretty close.

It is true that while a very skilled and scientific approach is observed in the making of whisky, there is still something very homely and rule-of-thumb about the whole process, which charmed my own artistic skill to the core. These are native ways I am talking about and what goes on beneath the kilt is no more mysterious than what goes on inside a copper still. This is alchemy of a high degree and it is no accident that these weird tubular objects of desire take on the characteristics of strange beasts and creatures from the time when hobgoblins and wizards cast spells and curses abroad like black confetti and ruled the dark areas of people's thoughts with the restricting fear of the unknown. Beneath this veil the heart of whisky was born, and it is no accident that it was so.

The early whisky distillers needed the very cover of darkness to mask their activities from the hooded eyes of excise men and their willing flunkies, the gaugers. These registered zombies roamed the Highlands and the Low-lands, like lost souls in Purgatory, searching for the liquid gold that was needed to line the coffers of the English throne, waging wars in foreign lands. Colonialism was a fever as deep-seated as the desire of the Gaelic soul to keep out the cold, and these forces matched each other face to face for supremacy.

The English won, of course, not because they were right, but because brute force and the English gentleman's god-given right to everything he claps his eyes on subdued the Scottish right to self-determination which, amongst other things, ushered in the Whisky Excise Act of 1823.

Although the Scots Parliament imposed considerable duty on whisky in 1644, it was in 1707, after the Union of the Parliaments, that the English Revenue Officers were allowed to cross the border. They attempted to control the rampant whisky distilling that was as much a part of Scottish tradition as hating the English. And so the trouble began.

It became a code of honour to make illicit whisky and it was a badge of honour and a blow struck against the English throne to drink it. It was also a nonsense to distillers and smugglers, all good men and true, that they should actually pay the sworn enemy for the privilege of making their own national drink, and a process that was as natural to them as it is now for the English to make jam and green tomato pickle. The travesty stuck in the throat of fervent patriots who realised that the duty paid, at hopelessly divergent rates, went to finance English land-rape worldwide – the Scotsmen rightly rebelled.

Even after a Royal Commission brought in the 1823 Act to stamp out the wild and rebellious practice of rampant distillation, true Scotsmen continued to insist on a smuggler's dram. It appears to make honourable, just and perfect sense. The Englishman's arrogant imposition was an abberation, and still is. The claim to this duty is probably illegal even today, but that's another story, and a claim I can only make here, since I think it would be foolish and futile to pursue it in the courts. Mind you, if there is a law student out there with enough balls to make it the subject of a thesis, who would I be to argue with him or her?

On the island of Islay, with 4,000 inhabitants on a piece of land 25 miles long by 20 miles wide, the 7 distilleries provide the British Government with 150 million pounds of duty annually. The people of Islay could, if they felt inclined, pull up the ladder and be self-sufficient, setting up their own principality, as prosperous and independent as Monaco, and screw the British Government. But instead the money is pissed away on foreign diplomatic mismanagement and every other government slush fund, by a Westminster long gone on rhyme or reason.

The first significant distiller to go legal was George Smith, grandson of a Bonnie Prince Charlie supporter, John Gow, who had changed his name to plain ole John Smith, to protect his family from the filthy wrath of the English after the Battle of Culloden. John became a farmer and whisky distiller but never went legal. His grandson, George, reckoned that legitimate distilling was the industry's future. He was encouraged in this thinking by his landlord, the penniless but land-rich Duke of Gordon, who stood to make good money from the sale of the grain grown on his land, which Smith transformed

into poetry and liquid assets. Consequently, George Smith was a turncoat in his fellow distillers' eyes. He became a controversial figure and was obliged to keep two pistols at the ready, day and night, for fear of reprisals. His company still flourishes under the name of The Glenlivet, in the Grampian Highlands of Speyside.

The Making of Whisky

But how is whisky made, this magical potion, this rare yet prolific nectar? Well, it is full of secrets we can never understand, but I *can* tell you how to make it. And why not? Who are these suits who thrash about spoiling it for others . . .

Basically, it is the simplest of culinary principles, couched in the old-fashioned ways of keeping the pot going on the hob and adding rich complexities of fresh new ingredients to an older brew. At least, that is how I perceived the origins of the process. It was probably an accident and maybe even goes back before the first known recorded reference to 'bolls of malt

enzyme diastase is produced in the barley during germination, which converts it to starch and sugar solubles. This is called 'Green Malt'. *YOU can simply spread yours on newspaper and turn it with your fingers, every hour on the hour, over a lazy weekend.*

Germination is halted by drying the converted barley in a malt kiln, a kind of pagoda-shaped tower, with a peat fire down below, allowing the smoke to rise up through the drying-floor which is covered with the barley, and then out into the open air through the pagoda-shaped chimneys. This process gives the raw material its peaty flavour. *YOU can achieve this on the average garden barbeque, using garden refuse, old leaves, peat moss etc. to*

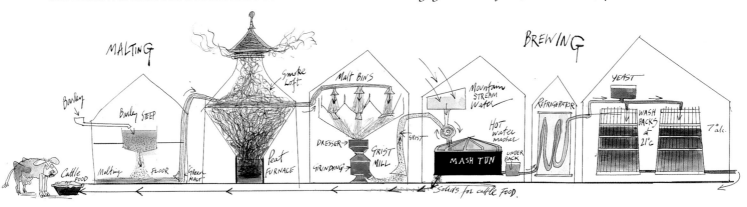

to Friar John Cor wherewith to make aquavitae', in the Scottish Exchequer Rolls of 1494. Probably old porridge, accidentally distilled on a reboil in a sock, oozed through an outlet pipe, under an ice-cold Highland stream, into an old leather sporran. A lost wandering Celtic Christian missionary may have spent his last words triggering the ingenuity of some restless, thirsty Scot with magical gibberish, of weird practices he had witnessed on board a junk on the South China Seas and Och aye Bingo! – the recipe was born.

The ingredients are *that* simple. Barley and pure, soft, Highland water bubbling over granite through peat, and yeast.

The barley goes through a malting process. It is steeped in water for two or three days, drained off, spread across a large stone or concrete malting floor and allowed to germinate. The germination is often controlled by determined Scottish insomniacs, ploughing it continually over a period of 8 to 12 days. The

smoke your grain dry, spread out on sheets of metal colander gauze.

The malt, now dried, is ground into grist, through a maroon-painted grist mill, still made by an engineering company called Porteus, who have made the same mill for over one hundred years. The resulting grist is mixed with hot water in a large circular tub called a mash tun. The soluble, powdery starch dissolves into a brownish, sugary, half-boiled liquid called wort, which is then drawn off, leaving behind husky solids. These husky solids, draff as they are now called, are used for cattle food. *YOU can use your kitchen blender on a slow speed, and use the discarded solids as compost nutrients.*

The wort is piped into a huge washback – another tub, which can hold anything from 9,000 to 45,000 litres, and is made of wood or, more frequently now, of stainless steel. This is fermented over a period of about 48 hours, with the addition of yeast at a temperature of around 21 degrees – 'the age a woman is at her most awkward,' as a Scottish misogynist said. The liquid, unattractively called wash, is now at about 7 degrees alcohol strength. The rest is still water and impurities. *YOU can use a plastic dustbin and maintain the temperature near a radiator in the hall, whilst the yeast goes to work and ferments the wash.*

Distillation takes place by boiling the wash in a copper still, shaped like an alchemist's retort. Alcohol boils at a lower temperature than water, and thus evaporates before the water does. The alcohol level of the distilled liquid rises to about 23 degrees in the vapour, which condenses into a liquid state, through a cooling plant of coiled pipes in cold water

ered whisky and it is still colourless. The rest, called feints, the tail of the distillation, is recycled and re-distilled, together with subsequent batches of wash and low wines, in skilfully balanced ways. It is this process which brought to mind the old country habit of the perpetual hot-pot over the open fire. What went before enriches what comes after and nothing is wasted, which to a Scotsman is second nature. Perhaps that is the real secret of the Scots' ability to produce the best malt whisky in the world – thrift.

Only when it has lain in oak sherry-casks, in a damp, cool cellar for at least three years, would a Scots' distiller presume to call it whisky. By then it will have lost any sharp-

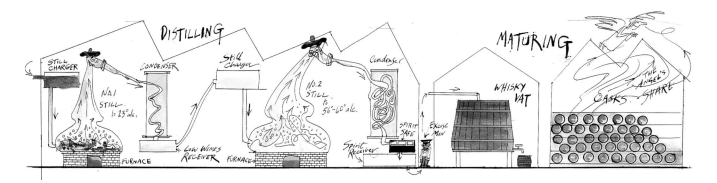

called a worm. The liquid, at this stage, is referred to as low wines. There are other types of condenser using parallel multi-pipes, but distillers still refer to it as the worm. *YOU can use an electric kettle, attaching central heating copper piping with solder to the spout – ask a plumber to do this work if you are not up to it, and he will coil it for you too. Submerge the coil in a sink or similar container of cold water, making use of gravity. Place another receptacle beneath the pipe to catch the low wines. Boil the kettle until dry. Pour it back into the kettle and boil it again but read on below first for technical procedure.*

The second distillation is a little tricky and this is where skill and innate traditional knowledge come into their own.

Only the middle fraction (middle cut) of this distillation is drawn off and passed through the spirit safe, by precise measure, to be stored and matured in casks. At this stage the alcoholic strength is between 53 and 60 degrees of ethanol. Ethanol is still not consid-

ness; it will have mellowed, and it will have absorbed the colour and some of the flavour from the oloroso sherry-soaked casks.

A percentage of the spirit will have evaporated during this time, and although this will pain a true Scotsman – not unreasonably – he philosophically refers to this loss as the angels' share. *YOU must be prepared to react in the same way, and while you are in jail, the result of your efforts can gently mature in some other dark, cool corner you may call your own, for a celebration on your release. How rich and mellow your particular distillation will turn out to be will depend on your cunning, native expertise, as much as the length of time you are inside. Five years, 10 years, 15, 25. That all depends on the judge and his particular preference. Judge Angus MacKnockaddu of Claplochshot Brae, for instance, liked a wee dram of 25 year-old straight from the cask after a trial. He is a hard but honourable man and if he can wait 25 years for a wee dram of your hard stuff, so can you, Aye!*

PREWHISKERY

A figure, little more than a headless torso, with two arms and two legs, crouched in mist on the edge of a bubbling cauldron. The cauldron belched and spluttered gaseous flaps of vapour into the atmosphere.

The figure breathed in deeply through two rude holes upon its shoulders to draw in the swirling ether and savour its strange and sulphurous aromas. It said to itself: 'One day I will learn to drink these vapours,' and it watched them through slime-eyed sockets. These swirling vapours embraced cold rocks and turned to liquid, dribbling and glistening in a murky light and falling through the figure's outstretched hands and onto the earth below. The figure lurched and shook with a soundless pleasure and smiled as only a featureless creature could. Its limbs buckled beneath it and it fell over and sank into a dreamlit sleep . . .

Ever since man learned to fashion a vessel that would not leak, he has sought to learn the secret of the vapours that would turn to intoxicating nectar, strong enough to drive reality into the deeper recesses of his mind and render him impervious to pain.

It was not an easy task. Through those timeless mists many faltered and fell before the gods of curiosity, whose blessings did not include mercy, for mercy was not in their estate. Curiosity was never a virtue. Curiosity is a hazardous adventure.

What Homo Torso had breathed in, through the glooping steam of countless natural distillations, merely triggered a desire beyond his comprehension and abilities. He could only watch in unrequited stupor.

But man was resolute and life was brutal. Even with the flickering rudiments of a dim intelligence, man knew instinctively that there must be something else in his existence other than abject misery and wretchedness. So, man stretched his curiosity to the limits of his ingenuity, whatever the awesome risks of failure. Somehow, he would fashion a magic potion to ward off the evil presence of his immediate discomfort, with invisible powers strong enough to release his dreams, and rise above himself to conquer the tyranny of his inevitable fate. It has been his problem and his salvation ever since.

Man first tried spit as a base material and ironically as an expression of how he truly felt about existence. He spat his puny contempt into a crucible and accumulated enough of it to ferment his rage. Indeed, it became an obsession, and an obstruction to progress, a diversion to fill a billion lives with futility. Evolution itself has staggered in man's stultifying stupors and left us, the inheritors, still struggling for some kind of purpose on this planet.

Wisdom has come and gone and we now behave like things which have only just stood up on two feet and grunted. We have always needed some kind of prop, and if it isn't spiritual faith we embrace, it is liquid vapours to drown the guilt and float in the tolerable lassitude of its power.

At man's awakening, I reckon, the deep desire to express broke the water of the womb he existed in, to cry out – to break the silence of repressed frustration. The primal scream was born of time's own long relentless torture. It was the breaking of bonds and the bursting out in birth of a new kind of man, of flesh but of the spirit too. The scream, at first, was garbled and without form. The earth screamed back and caused the rivers and the flood of fresh new streams of life, each with a hunger and appetite to suit itself.

Man created his own mouth, I've heard tell – a sudden gape to utter what he would.

Yet, there was nothing to say except to croak despair and probably all he had been denied in thirst. Until he drank, how could he know what to express? He gutted every open hole for liquid he had only seen and smelled. So, he sucked and spewed, and sucked again. So much he had to learn and when he gorged amongst the rocks of his twilight ancestors who had been denied and only dreamed of what thirst might be, he learned to spit and retch, for what he thought was nectar from the nasal gods of tantalising odours which had fired those dreams of wetness, turned rancid to the palate, an uncrafted aberration and a mockery of its glistening promise.

His mouth shattered all he held sacred. It mocked him with its taste buds and screamed the brutal truth like a bleeding wound. But now there was the appetite that would not go away. At once a rich new vein of exploitation inside himself awoke – and a Hell hole – craving satisfaction. There he stood, the poor and wretched devil of his own devices.

Here endeth the first lesson . . .

The real clue appeared in Peru. Not Peru as we know it now, the grisled fetid waters, lapping around the flyblown ankles of trusting children, in love with life, and eager to gorge on its poisons, but the Peru of pure water, dappling in shade and plunging down ravines in God's own laboratory, a garden of Eden glowing in shafts of sunlit signals. There was a life to be had, where all men grew like animals. They ate what was there and drank what flowed out of cracks in the earth. It was a time of innocent indulgence.

But, then, there came those who took what was there and created an experience which awakened taste buds, hitherto lying

On the following pages: 'Across the flat plains of Nazca, man devised and drew his vast plans for the creation of vessels in which to foment a potable substance to gratify more than a mere thirst.'

dark and damp in the deep recesses of primeval memory. They came and they tasted the juice of fruit off the tree, breathed in the pungent smells of its decomposition, and the filtered moistures off bare rocks. They said to themselves, 'This can only be the beginning'.

Such men are hallowed – and such men are cursed, for that which man ingeniously forged out of these soft waters and the produce of the earth, was a double-edged sword, a rod for mankind's back, and a nectar to choose for those rarer moments in life, when only the thrust and massage of something electrifying will suffice.

Across the flat plains of Nazca, man devised and drew his vast plans for the cre-

ation of vessels in which to foment a potable substance to gratify more than a mere thirst. Mysterious diagrams evolved across hundreds of square miles of the sacred plateau, for no effort was spared in the quest to find the utensil of the exact shape with which to extract the elixir that, up until then, lived only in the catacombs of ignorance.

Amongst the symbols of birds, monkeys, crocodiles, spiders, astronauts, alpacas, and all the creatures of man's experience, which he lovingly described, there looms the undeniable shape of a magic crucible and the coiled worm of discovery. Without the worm all efforts would have been in vain. Whatever waters and wherever the base fruits of the earth, Nazca man needed a worm to cool the potent steams moofling off a bubbling bowl of half-intoxicating soup, known as mash, a boiled compilation of anything fermentable . . . birds, monkeys, crocodiles, spiders, astronauts, alpacas, and llamas. Particularly llamas. Llama spitting, a particularly nauseous habit of these irresistibly beautiful creatures, which seduce an admirer within a range of anything up to ten yards, flutters its eyelids coquettishly, and – splat! – covers the unsuspecting victim in a glutin of masticated hay and coca leaves. It is an emblem of good luck for those so spat upon, and a source of raw, enzyme-rich grist for fermentation and distillation.

Llamas can be provoked to spit like automatic rifles and therefore provocateurs were employed. They had to be nimble, so most of the jobs went to the young men who were nifty enough to step aside and catch the precious fluid in chicha jugs, still used today to pass around the local mescal, usually with

the worm in it for the lucky imbiber. The worm in this instance would be an afterthought, a kind of juicy dimension to a distilled spirit (spitr!, students of semantics, please note), rather in the way fruit, cherries, and so on are pickled in spirit, to create a delectable titbit, to restimulate the palate after drinking and eating orgies. The body needs food at such times. Coca, incidentally, is to Peruvian Indians the imparter of continuous force rather than a temporary spur to help one over an immediate emergency. Indians to whom whisky has been given have been known to declare: 'Coca helps a man to live, and whisky makes him row a boat.' Figure that one out. I found it deep with philosophical significance.

But, the Peruvian Indians needed to know about distillation, and, importantly, about the transformation into a potable substance of their raw material which grew in such abundance, but which still required treatment

POT-STILL MAN. ROCK PAINTING, Hawker, Southern Australia

MOCHE WARRIOR. PERU

before it was ready for total extraction of its properties. In whisky, the transformation is germination of the raw material, barley, and in primitive cultures it is very often mastication of the raw material to hand, namely coca. Since llamas and other cud-chewing species masticate more than man, which is in fact constantly, they have been employed as the instruments of man's desires. The spitting is therefore not considered unpleasant so much as necessary. The Peruvians even make a coca wine, which is regarded not so much as a stimulant, but a tonic, possessing not only immediate, but also lasting effects. Alcohol has been pursued through the ages not merely because of its intoxicating powers, but far more importantly as an elixir of life.

It is this motivation, this deeper psychological subterranean drive of primitive man to deify his own particular creative spirit, which grabs my interest, far more than the mere evolution of a drink, with its sole purpose of obfuscating the mind. Distilled spirits have a darker character, a complex personality and a compulsive demand for ownership. Wine has a Bacchanalian abandon in its nature and touches life lightly with joy. Spirit is like a genie which, when released, can unlock the magical uncertainties of the unknown and beckon us towards a voyage of dangerous intensity. The emphasis is entirely different.

Civilisation has advanced only by the adoption of primitive means and to even hazard a guess about the why's and wherefore's of any particular practice in any given culture can only lead to the surprising possibility that you may just as well be right and your fantasy is, in fact, within the bounds of possibility. At least it encourages artistic licence of a very entertaining calibre and I am not about to argue with that. Otherwise I am undone.

It has usually been the Church or governing bodies, seeing no possibility of exacting revenue from known stimulants, who discourage their use, particularly if such substances have superstitious associations. Often these raw materials are cited as having a pro-vocative purpose in the practice of idolatory and are therefore damned as being evil and debilitating. Therefore, they are used by primitive people simply because they are too ignorant to know any better. It was only when the Spanish Conquistadors discovered that they got more work out of their Indian slaves when they were chewing coca leaves that they actively encouraged its use, since it was in effect paying dividends. Both parties were happy. The Indians have been known to rely entirely on the chewing of coca* leaves for days without the need for food or drink because, quite simply, it prevented the feeling of hunger, thirst, loss of strength and even kept them free of disease.

One way or another, laws have evolved to encourage habits imbued with deep social significance – whilst providing huge revenue for the national coffers – as long as the end result has not caused a total breakdown or insurrection. Hence the dilemma of present day governments of increasingly health conscious societies who attempt to balance the books by imposing massive duty on certain condoned subtances whilst appearing to condemn them self-righteously with superficial controls in public places.

Darwin established that organic life tends to increase beyond its means of subsistence, and balance is maintained effectively only by the survival of the fittest. The Spanish finally declared war on the coca plant because of its deep superstitious significance and, in their desperation to stamp it out as a species, instead exterminated a whole race who held it sacred.

*The Incas regarded coca as a symbol of divinity, and, originally, its use was confined exclusively to the Royal Family. Were it ever thus! The bestowing of a gift of coca upon a guest was a high mark of esteem. It was also accepted by a vanquished foe as a sign of subjection to an Inca chief who had conquered him.

Ralph STEADman

Cave Paintings

Between 10,000 and 40,000 years ago, at the end of the last ice age, Cro-magnon man left many marks of significance on the cave walls of Les Eyzies in South West France, the Gargas caves in the French Pyrenees, Lascaux, Niaux, Rouffignac, Altamira in Spain and Sungir, near Moscow. He was recording his existence at the end of a twilight era of early Homo Erectus, or perhaps the beginnings of a species, known generally as modern man.

Many of the symbols are mysterious; some are self-explanatory. The hand-stencils were probably a signature, since no other form of writing existed, and are perhaps a way of suggesting that these artworks were done by hand.

But some symbols, it has to be said, have the appearance of vessels used for the fermentation and distillation of intoxicating potions, made from the droppings of mammoths and the dribblings of bison.

After the brutality of mere survival, man had time to occupy himself with other pursuits. Art and drink, therefore, manifestly demonstrated themselves, within his marks of intention, around his place of habitation. The intellectual and the spiritual had already assumed a serious aspect of a life to be lived to the full.

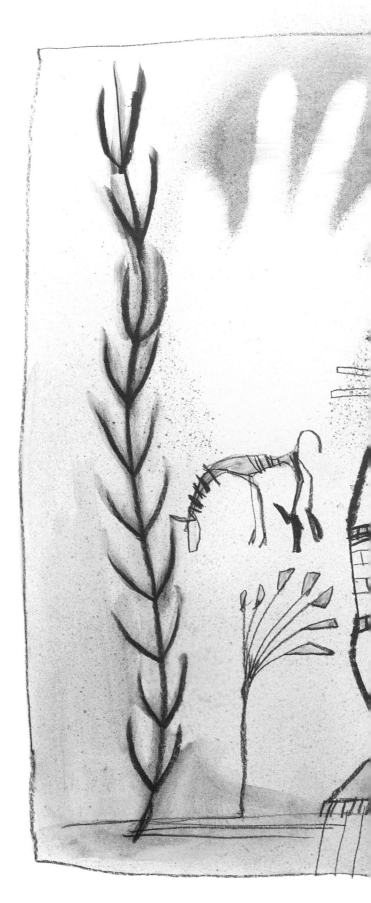

The second recorded pot still in history.

Aborigines

NGUNGUNDA FIGURE WITH HANGOVER. North-Western AUSTRALIA

So, where were we? Distillation, where it came from? Why, if, and who? If you need to know about a people and their closest thoughts and activities, look at their art. Art is the repository of all man's expression and all he reveres and holds sacred.

The aborigines, whose way of life goes back uninterrupted for 40,000 years, show in their art examples of a kind of spiritual disembodiment. Figures float in intoxicated abandon. Amongst the hunters and the gatherers, however, there are examples of observed animal forms. These bear no evidence of spiritual possession and appear strangely 'normal'. They are, in fact, near-perfect examples of anatomical correctness, as though it were inconceivable that an animal would possess a spiritual life or, indeed, feelings of any kind

whatsoever. Only in snake forms has the aboriginal artist imbued the creature with a kind of supernatural power and spiritual significance. His art abounds with intricate worm spirals which wind hypnotically across a surface and develop almost into a significant texture with their own powers, in their own right. Man, however, is portrayed possessed, and full of imaginings. Some figures seem to be in the throes of serious hangovers, appearing helpless and invariably in the squatting position. Some float angelically and soar into a world of dreams, whilst others, notably the 'wondjina' figures of North West Australia, are invariably rendered in the recumbent posture together with other heads – the 'children of the wondjinas' – or the souls of men who have been released into the world again by some intoxicating experience. A wondjina is considered to be an anthropomorphic figure and the bringer of rain. It is associated with the beginnings of heaven and earth, which to an aboriginal has always been there. In the bowels of the earth there lives *Ungud*, the creator of all things and all life, to which all men return after death, to be reborn.

Ungud is portrayed as a snake, which probably accounts for the importance of the worm patterns which appear everywhere, and which have absolutely nothing to do with the distillation process whatsoever. But you never know for sure.

We are led to believe by cosmologists that there are black holes in space which represent the infinite compression of matter, caused by the big bang, the moment of creation and the resulting expansion of the universe. Now, there are even wrinkles in time, a side-effect of such a release of energy. Well, OK. I'll go along with that.

And so, Ungud is identified with the earth and all the earth we see is simply the back of Ungud – a huge snake, which is also a symbol of water, the passing of time and man's state of mind. Ungud 'finds' the first wondjina in a creative dream at the bottom of a waterhole. Every spring and waterhole in North West Australia has its wondjina figure situated nearby, usually floating on an overhanging rock, where ordinary men cannot lie down.

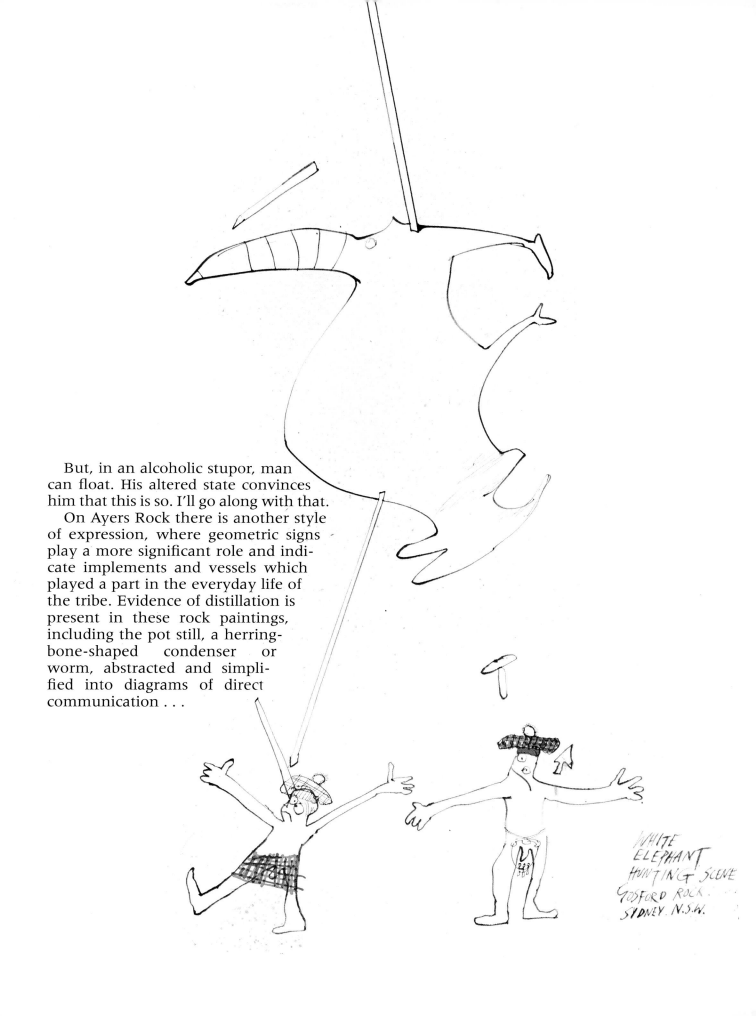

But, in an alcoholic stupor, man can float. His altered state convinces him that this is so. I'll go along with that.

On Ayers Rock there is another style of expression, where geometric signs play a more significant role and indicate implements and vessels which played a part in the everyday life of the tribe. Evidence of distillation is present in these rock paintings, including the pot still, a herring-bone-shaped condenser or worm, abstracted and simplified into diagrams of direct communication . . .

WHITE ELEPHANT HUNTING SCENE GOSFORD ROCK. SYDNEY. N.S.W.

Arnhem Land Rock Art depicting a Mimi spirit in the form of a stylistic monochrome stick figure. The Mimi are harmless spirits with a sense of mischief. They are tall and need to protect themselves against strong winds. Otherwise they float *away. When aborigines first arrived in Arnhem Land between 10,000 and 18,000 years ago the Mimi were already living there, but became the paintings and inhabited the rocks, having their separate culture, similar to humans, but inside*

the rock world. Drinking was one of their activities and throwing up the spirit of themselves expressed a dynamic result of self-indulgence. This is depicted abstractly by a series of lines and dashes. The small rodent-like figure around the bowel area of the Mimi portrays the fact that the Mimi was rat-arsed and paying for his excesses dearly. Such works were not taken seriously, though considered to be an example to their descendants of what would happen after too much imbibing.

Sumerians

SUMERIAN STILL IN THE SHAPE OF THE
GODDESS ISHTAR — daughter of SIN and
ANU. She was the divine personification
of the planet VENUS.

All great civilisations developed and flourished in river valleys. The earliest cultivators of the flood plain between the Tigris and the Euphrates, the land of Babylon, milk and honey, or Iraq as it is now known, were the Sumerians, and the Semites, the Akkadians to the north. Nobody really knows who is the older of the two races, only that there seems to have been some turmoil between them and cross-pollination over the centuries.

In spite of themselves they created a system of irrigation which transformed the plain between the two rivers into a Garden of Eden. Food surpluses proliferated into food mountains galore, and their own local city gods were idolised for being so generous. They gave private audiences to worthy citizens and had them force-fed publicly for all to witness the gods' benificence.

Gluttony became fashionable, and obesity an outward sign of devotion. Sumerian women, and Sumerian men, too, developed enormous bottoms, vast floating bulges of unwanted flesh, great sagging walloods of

pocket-creased blubber. It was only made bearable by the local gods, who said it was OK to worship fat gods, but it got so that nobody could fall to his knees and worship, without finding it impossible to get up again. People who tried, rolled over onto their backs, and the streets were full of worshippers, rocking helplessly like great overturned turtles.

Something was desperately needed to absorb the cornucopia of fruit and veg tumbling onto the population, not to stultify the abundance, but to extract the essence from such an embarrassment of riches, and preserve it for later. It was the fat bottoms that held the answer. The alembic shape of even the most modest corpulentee gave the Sumerians the idea of honouring their fat local gods in the form of strange pot stills. In this cunning way they did not cause offence. Instead, the people worshipped the very shapes their craftsmen wrought and placed them on high plinths so that they did not have to go down on their knees and get stuck in a supplicating posture.

By 3000 BC, it was all in hand, and godlike effigies had been devised to transform all their voluptuous goodies into rare and intoxicating liqours. So fervent were the Sumerians not to have to kneel again, that their gods found themselves worshipped on manmade mountains called Ziggurats, enclosing vast underground pot stills. But I digress . . .

Olmec Hunchback Pot Still depicting various physical deformities and facial paralysis as often happens to inebriates in a drunken stupor. La VENTA, TABASCO 1000 BC. Not the peaceful folk history gave them for so long, seem more recent to be the NAHUAS, the top up their captives [and] bounce them like balls down PYRAMID steps and attempted to avert their blood as an offering to their gods.

The Tincturer at his Tinct. (He works instinctively.)

CEYLON

A rude still, employed in Ceylon for medicinal spirits, was more like a petrified python than a worm. It became a built-in piece of architecture, treated as an altar with a serious purpose, and yet it was managed by a smiling, humourless drunk. The tinctures it moofled off became the very lodestone of health-preserving prescriptions and led the field in body-restoratives, before there was even anything resembling a shop to be seen.

INDONESIA

In Indonesia the first inklings of Celtic distillation bubbled up through the land mass joining continents which were fast disintegrating and moving apart. The Celts staggered off in the direction of India and Asia looking for a place to call their own. Unwanted, hungry and above all thirsty, they moved on like compulsive nomads.

INDIA

The art of distillation is believed to go back even further in the history of India and fermentation and distillation were considered to be the bedrock of all medical science. It is probable that the Celts, who passed through India about that time, carelessly left the idea behind on a rock. Indians, however, did not practise the quaffing of such potions in large quantities but administered them as tinctures for the treatment of specific ailments. These same tinctures are still peddled today in little brown bottles with commercial conviction at worthy health shops and in herbalists' consulting rooms.

In the ancient culture of Maya, sarcophagi were often an excuse for expressing an appetite for the the life to come. Sarcophagus reliefs from the tomb of the temple of inscriptions in Palenque, a Mayan city in the Yucatan, display figures in repose similar to the Mayan rain-god Chacmool. Chacmool was a thirsty god and demanded pure water or the children of the people. Kings would demand aqua vitae, the water of life, to sustain them in the eternal life to come, and, therefore, their desire is personified in the Mayan pot still which feeds their craving.

Chacmool, the thirsty Mayan rain-god.

MAYAN
HANGOVER
MASKS, EL MIRADOR
150BC—A.D 150.

Ralph STEADman

Above: Mayan Hangover Masks, El Mirador, 150 BC to AD 150 . No man wished to show his weakness following serious long-drawn out festivities by appearing in a diminished state the morning after. A solid month of merrymaking and offerings to the gods can leave a body ravaged, ripped and no better than sea-blanched flotsam washed up on a lonely beach. A mask of opulent, optimistic brilliance declared strength, a defiant hope for the future and disguised magnificently an otherwise destroyed and pathetic specimen.

Right: The cheekiest wee dram ever to lean against a cut stone in the temple of Apollo and seek sanctuary in Aphrodite's bath. Blunter than a brush seller's foot in the door, it strobes itself into your living room and positions itself horizontally on your best sofa in muddy boots.
'Got anything to drink? ' it says, as it reaches for the electronic channel selector and clicks on a game show.
'Aw shit! Ain't you got a Sky dish?'
You haven't, obviously, because Cyprus Whisky has moved through to your drawing room and tries to fix your hi-fi.
'Got something a little less radical than Tony Bennett, Guy Mitchell or Frankie Lane?'
Unfortunately no, I never went downmarket. I always encouraged quality and finesse.

NEFERTITI presents offerings to her GOD ATEN. EGYPTIAN DISTILLATION or PURIFICATION of the SPIRIT of DUAMUTEF* one of the FOUR SONS of HORUS, and protector of the STOMACH... EIGHTEENTH DYNASTY. *JACKAL-HEAD.

EGYPT

The Sky Goddess Nut holds up the Sky as Geb, the Earth God tries to reach her. They have been separated by Ra, the Sun God and sovereign of the sky. Shu, the Goddess of the Atmosphere, is distilled in spirit and holds Nut aloft attempting to keep them apart, helped by her handy manservant, Forbitu. Distilled spirits separated the Egyptians from reality and held their lives in the balance until they returned to Earth. The wily jackal, Duamutef, son of Horus and guardian of the Stomach pretends to look away and hold the balance in check. He is helpless, and unable to intervene. 21st Dynasty. 1102–952 B.C.

Meanwhile, the Egyptians constructed vast pot stills in the desert, to create enough nectar for the gods to last for eternity.

In their art are examples of such utensils, showing Nefertiti presenting offerings to her god, Aten, depicting Egyptian distillation or purification of the spirit of Duamutef, who was the jackal-headed son of Horus, worshipped as protector of the stomach. Many wall decorations repeat the symbol of the Egyptian pot still, and Queen Hapshepsut had her temple adorned with them, in the Valley of the Kings, 1,500 years before the birth of Christ.

She was a power-hungry demon-Queen – that is to say, she was as bad as the men, only a bit more cunning, as she needed to be to survive.

Hapshepsut was the first woman Pharoah. For 1,000 years before her, drinks were fermented from pumpkins and water melons, figs, dates, grapes, pomegranates and wild berries. Brewing is pictured on the walls of tombs as early as the 5th Dynasty (2500 BC). Loaves of bread made from wheat or barley were baked and allowed to ferment in water.

The Sky Goddess Nut holds up the sky as Geb, the Earth God, tries to reach her. They have been separated by Ra, the Sun God, and sovereign of the sky. Shu, the Goddess of the Atmosphere, is distilled in spirit and holds Nut aloft, attempting to keep them apart, helped by her handy manservant, Forbitu. Distilled spirits separated the Egyptians from reality and held their lives in the balance until they returned to earth. The wily jackal, Duamutef, son of Horus and Guardian of the Stomach, pretends to look away while holding the balance in check. He is helpless and unable to intervene. 21st Dynasty, 1102–952 BC.

The distillation of such a mash would have been used for medicinal purposes, and all distilled spirits played that significant role in ancient cultures.

Sacred Vulture-Headed Distillation Still of the Goddess Mut – wife of Amon.

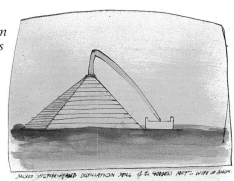

Sacred Vulture-headed distillation still of the goddess Mut – wife of Amon.

Egyptian pot stills. Wall decoration – Queen Hapshepsut, Temple at Deir El-Bahri, Valley of the Kings. 18th Dynasty, 1505–1484 BC. Power-hungry and devious, she blocked the very young Tuthmosis III's accession and mounted Pharaoh's throne herself. Beer brewing goes back beyond the 5th dynasty (2500 BC) when wheat and barley loaves were fermented in water. Distillation was an easy step from that – purification of the spirit.

Osiris, the great god – first king of Egypt and Great Pharoah, has perfumes distilled from aromatic flowers. It is doubted whether the Egyptians had discovered distillation. Egyptians had no electricity but the great burial chambers were not adorned by the light of candle or oil lamps since the artists and craftsmen would have asphyxiated in the enclosures in which they were working. The sun god Rah gave them the idea – they used the Gods' light, the light of the sun, which they reflected off shining metal shields, guiding the rays down into the deep tunnels towards another slave holding a similar shield who would bounce the light onwards towards the place of work and the tomb itself. They were ingenious.

The Egyptians in the time of Dioclesian (AD 205–305) were really heavy boozers. They told the Babylonians who told the Hebrews. A heavily sedated foot messenger transmitted the news to Thrace, whereupon a travelling Celt peddling belt buckles and leather accessories mentioned it in Spain to a bull wrestler and gall merchant who was on his way to Gaul in the hope that the Gauls had a use for it. It intrigued the ancient Greeks as knowledge. The Romans preferred wine. But the Arabians in deepest, darkest times, as did the Egyptians, distilled perfumes and aromatic waters (people have got drunk on Chanel No.5). The word 'alcohol' is Arabic originally and meant 'fine powder', gradually becoming 'essence' and then 'pure spirit'.

EGYPTIAN POT STILLS: Wa
(1505-1484 B.C.) Eighteenth Dynast
mounted PHARAOH's throne herself
+ BARLEY loaves were fermented in w

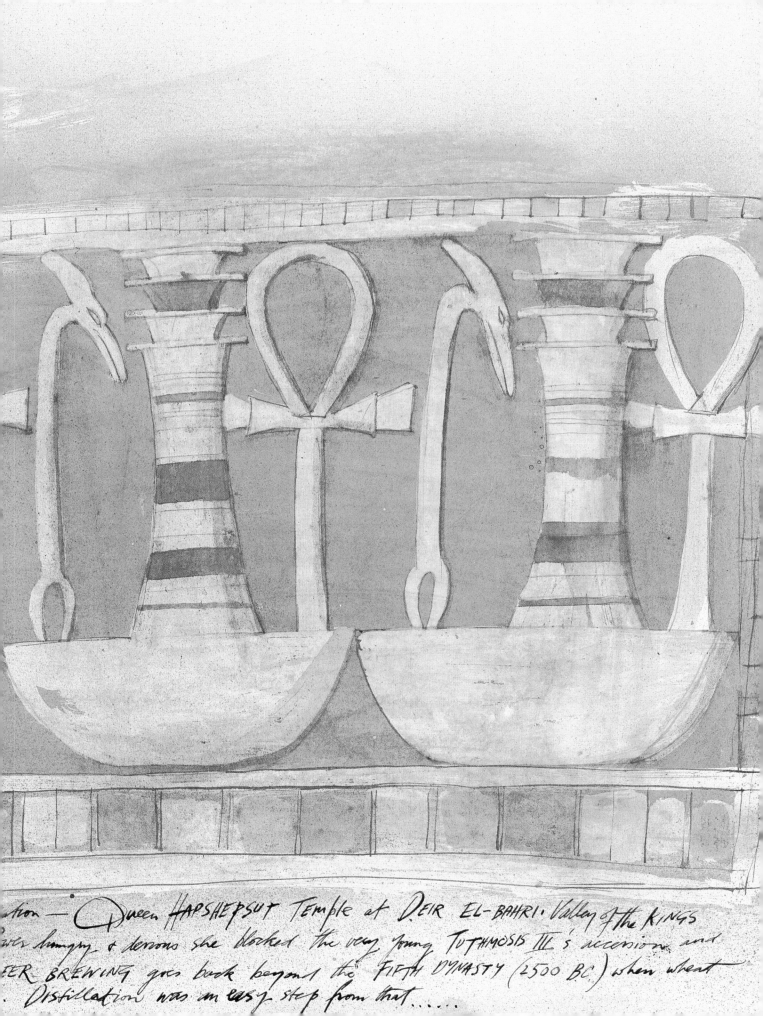

ation — Queen HAPSHEPSUT Temple at DEIR EL-BAHRI. Valley of the KINGS
was hungry & serious she blocked the very young TUTHMOSIS III's accession and
EER BREWING goes back beyond the FIFTH DYNASTY (2500 B.C.) when wheat
Distillation was an easy step from that......

Greeks and ROMANS ΓΡΕΕΚΣ ανδ ΡΟΜΑΝΣ

Dioscorides was a physician during the reign of Nero (AD 54–68) who investigated the medicinal properties of plants, distilling all potable substances and writing his observations down in a work called *Materia Medica*. He extracted quicksilver from cinnobar also but that was only a suicide's drink.

He is depicted in an illustrated Arabic translation of the 13th century, preparing a potion for an ailing noble, in a strange goldfish bowl-shaped vessel, boiling over a small enclosed furnace, and drawing off the steam through a long tube. It appears that he hasn't quite got the hang of distillation, because most of his steam is escaping through the open space at the top, and not much is finding its way through the tube. I only mention this in case readers think I am merely imposing some sort of wish-fulfilment on my version of how things may have been. In the pic-

ture he is definitely boiling his concoction, his wort, in an attempt to capture its restorative properties, by enticing the vapours to rise up the tube he is holding. This may only be the simplistic stylisation of the Arabian artist who was being diagrammatic in order to convey what was happening in as simple a way as possible.

Did the Greeks and Romans know about distillation? Yes. The Greeks did, but the Romans chose wine as their tipple.

Xenophon (430–354 BC), talks of barley and water in his great work, *Anabasis*, which records the retreat of thousands of Greeks across Asia Minor, who distilled their disappointments into a refined philosophy of life, known as Humanism, a philosophy which realises, primarily, that man is more than a mere passage for food. He is also a serious drinker who needs spiritual sustenance of

rare and intoxicating, intellectual vapours.

The Greeks were not troubled by despotic rulers. They were preoccupied with the nature of the world around them and the processes of life. The arts and sciences were indivisible and worked in harmony as part of life's natural pattern.

Thales of Miletus, who lived around 640 to 546 BC, considered that all objects on the earth – buildings, togas, mountains, utensils, wheels and drinking vessels – were made up of one variously arranged substance, water. He was wrong, but he was on the right track, which Democritus clarified around 400 BC.

He stated that the universe is made up of millions of atoms, arranged in different ways to create the nature of objects and, indeed, life itself.

But the water theory was the stuff of visionaries. Thales of Miletus was a bothy man before his time, a distiller before he had yet grasped the concept. He had a sixth sense that the transformation of water into another yet undreamed-of experience was merely a matter of time.

The Romans, while being rather fond of orgiastic consumption, preferred the gentler Bacchanalian delights of wines. Their preference persisted well into the Dark Ages. A serious interest in the restorative powers of distilled spirits could well have prevented the Roman Empire from declining when it did. Armies fired on drams of aqua vitae could probably have held the barbarians off for at least another thousand years and changed the course of history, or at least kept it on the course it was on.

Olympus Bottle Dance

DARK AGES

But the Dark Ages arrived and quackery, lawlessness, deprivation, looting, rape and pillage blossomed, like rampant cholera. Not that it did not under the Romans, but *they* carried on a more controlled rape and pillage programme, under the rule of law and democratic tyranny.

The Gauls were vanquished throughout Western Europe, scholars were put to the sword, and much ancient wisdom was lost, or simply disappeared from view for 500 years or so. Only missionary monks read and wrote, travelling like god-protected beings and preserving the written word and the ideas of the ancient Greeks and earlier Romans, locking it all away behind monastery walls. Ironically, it was the small, persecuted but persistent Jewish sect in a tiny corner of the Roman Empire who were instrumental in keeping alive the concept of teaching, at first resisted brutally by the Romans as a dangerous form of insurrection against the godlike Caesars.

Nevertheless, Christianity sustained learning and wisdom beyond its own doctrines, and enabled these oases of religious contemplation also to protect every last vestige of human activity from the fashionable desire to slash and burn, and from certain oblivion inside the looming darkness.

The crafty monks had not forgotten that man does not live by mead alone, and, since he and she read in Latin, kept stumbling across a couple of words of great significance: Aqua Vitae, or Water of Life. That may be only a tenuous thread of reason, but reason enough to look into and revive what might at that time have been lost or forgotten in the darkness and swirling mists of rank stupidity and boorish behaviour.

During the Dark Ages, apart from bumping into one another (the electric light had not yet been invented, remember), superstitions were developed into sciences. Everything was found then and everything was lost. Only Humanism was left to be rediscovered. The barbarians proved too numerous and insistent for a Roman Empire, dying on the inside from the internal struggles of power-hungry politicians attempting to recreate the absolute power of Augustus Caesar. Anything that represented organisation simply sank beneath a tidal wave of disruption and decay. The barbarians, made up of Goths, Vandals, Franks, Burgundians, Angles, Saxons, Jutes and, of course, Celts, were fleeing the ferocity of Tartar-Mongolian Huns, the vodka drinkers.

My favourites, the Visigoths and the Ostrogoths, were real buggers. The volatile emotions of all these maniacs could no longer be contained, and the whole of Central Europe erupted in a similar way to the Eastern European tragedy exploding today after the rapid disintegration of cohesive Communism. However, by AD 500 things got really dark and to get any kind of drink at all was a bonus. Boiled bone brandy was a big favourite, and goat's devilhorn Brooth was another. Fetid Gristle Curd, distilled through the five stomachs of a cow, drove warriors, already hungry for blood, into a frothing maelstrom of uncontrollable rage. Human sacrifices were a great source of raw material, and one leg, mixed with the bone jelly of five hundred chicken legs, kept a marauding horde insane for a week.

What a tragic loss! These people could not read or write, so they never wrote the recipes down. Hundreds of rich and elegant potions were lost forever.

When Rome finally succumbed and caved in, all those weird and wonderful liquors were just a memory to the Visigoths and Vandals who began to adopt Roman ways. They embraced Christianity, married their women and, only then, learned to read and write, when it was too late to change their mind. They decked themselves out in the clothes of the Empire, like crude caricatures of the Roman way of life, but without the substance. They listened to the Pope, liked what he said, and started drinking sacramental wine. Their own bizarre concoctions fell on hard times. Barbarian liquor peddlers started fermenting grapes, just like the Romans, and then distilling those.

At first their old habits died hard, and wild

Sadak and the WATERS of OBLIVION

This is a Persian legend of a young man, who, because of his intense wish for a good world, finally loses his sense of optimism and goes in search of a place, foretold by a genie, who promised him an elixir to ease his pain of disillusionment. This place contains the Waters of Oblivion, distilled from intense natural forces which, between them, create a pure and magical potion which can transport the imbiber to a New World of beauty, love and eternal peace.

Sadak gets lost and thinks he is in Hell because he cannot see anything but turmoil. In fact, what he is looking for is produced by such violent forces, which are, in fact, all around him, that he cannot imagine the Waters of Oblivion to be in such a place.

The Dark Ages envelop him and he wanders helplessly on, determined, but also dying for lack of the aqua vitae to restore his vision of a better world.

PERSIANS

For centuries, until he
developed the alembic, man
struggled to understand why
his vapours evaporated into
thin air. He evolved the right
shape, but, at first, used it the
wrong way round.

The Persians got it nearly
right when they used the
same shape, turned it the
right way up and sat in it,
with their heads out of the top
to take a bath. The sweat
from Sultans, Califs, Sultanas
and other eminent bodies was
condensed into jewelled
containers, fermented, and
then distilled into an early
form of spirit, called Arak,
which was eventually
dropped in favour of palm
juice, rice and molasses.

So precious a discovery
was reserved for the
renovation of the body in its
decrepit old age, until the first
recorded drunk in history
tried to describe his bodily
sensations after an eight-day
bender (see picture), and
launched man onto a helter-
skelter ride of wild and
degenerate binges.

boar brains, slave offal and porcupine thighs were ceremoniously added to the mash, to suit a barbarian palate. As time went on, complaints about the crude flavours, once the nectar of louts, became offensive and even life-threatening. Orgies became an ordeal and frenzies of wretching caused terrible disruptions and harrowing sights, unbecoming of the new civilised ways. Barbarian distillates were severely modified and some even banned. Only the Celts maintained the base approach to the old ways, much further north.

The darkness became a boon. Such practices are better kept from the eyes of mortal man. If you know what is in things you would probably never touch them, let alone eat or drink them. It was the Celts who moved on and left the whimpering Visigoths to endure the apathy of their newly acquired and suffocating civilisation.

The Franks (Merovingians) sprawled their kind across the old Roman province of Gaul and developed the art of winemaking, though they, too, pursued the vapours, transforming the draff of crushed grape-skins and pips into their own kind of soulful despair called eau-de-vie.

From the aniseed plant they created a kind of green suicide called absinthe which has retained a subterranean remoteness to this day. The absinthe drinker is supposed to live in a romantically tragic, twilight zone of his or her own devices, and is linked with some of the great writers and artists of the late 19th century and La Belle Epoque.

Charlemagne (AD 768 – 814), with the backing of Catholic Rome, conquered and converted the pagan Saxons of central Germany, south and east of the Vosges, into Christians, but into beer-swilling Christians, a kind of defiant protest on their part, and they still drink half-fermented brews that provoke the kind of intestinal eruptions that can empty rooms.

They, too, developed their own kind of distillates from whatever came to hand and were anything but grapes. Blue plums, apricots, cherries, strawberries, raspberries, and pears were transformed into 'Wassers' and 'Geists' of organised complexity which now go under the generic title of schnapps.

The Dutch used juniper berries, adding a variety of herbs, fruit and spices, such as coriander seed, angelica root, cinnamon bark, liquorice, nutmeg and orange peel, to make a base spirit which they call 'moutwyn', dutch gin or genever.

Although distillation was well advanced during the dark age of all countries, it was the Arabs who initiated the lands they had conquered into their own heretical arts and beliefs.

Alchemy

Among the Arabian arts and sciences which seemed particularly threatening to the now tightly-knit Christian unit of Europe, was the process of distillation, known as Alchemy, or the Black Art. It held a great fascination for some, who believed it was possible to transmutate all base metals into gold. The Greeks had attempted it, and so had the Egyptians.

*Abucasis was the first Western philosopher to teach the art of
distillation. Philosophy and distillation have much in
common. From a mash tun full of words, wisdom is distilled.
From a mash tun of worts whisky is distilled.
13th-century Arnoldus de Villa Nova, a chemist and
physician, describes distilled spirit and its effects: 'It moveth
some to excessive outbursts and some it leads to vigour and
creative ecstasy – this water of life.'*

The serpent and the salamander became symbolic, and are often depicted consuming themselves by swallowing their tails first, and, in effect, distilling their very beings into something concentrated and pure. It is even suggested that the creation of the world happened through this very process of the vapourising and distilling of floating matter, consuming itself by becoming serpent-like heads and tails and therefore disappearing inside itself. (Thales of Miletus would probably have agreed with that idea.)

The right idea . . . the wrong way round.

In the Street of the Alchemists in Prague, alchemy, black magic and the occult were practised. Doctor Faustus allegedly forfeits his soul to Mephistopheles, in exchange for one perfect moment, in this very street – a distillation of perfect happiness.

Those alchemists who lost occult inspiration, and devoted themselves to purely material research, were treated as inflated charlatans, or souffleurs, the prototypes of modern-day chemists. Souffleurs, rather like drug companies today, became preoccupied with the pursuit of gold rather than wisdom. Their equipment reflected much of the non-sensical quackery surrounding the quasi-mystical aura of the alembic, the basic utensil for the distillation of anything tangible.

Superstition, fired by this scientific facade, transformed anybody with half a brain into a mystic or visionary overnight (not unlike the effect this Apple Mac computer has on its operator who thinks that the meaning of life is hidden somewhere in one of its wretched little icons). The height of madness was reached when it was thought possible to create life, without sexual intercourse, by the distillation of the four elements, resulting in

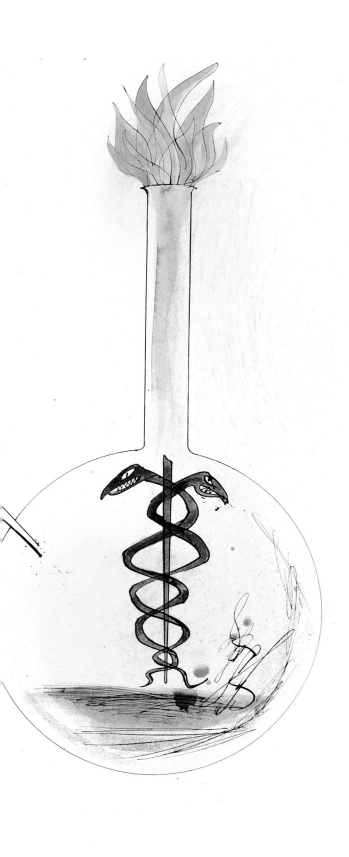

the union of opposites, a child of the mind, called a Homunculus.

The birth must take place in an hermetically-sealed flask, creating an hermaphrodite, an androgynous being of both male and female characteristics, who is supposed to watch over the beginning and the end of all things, including magic and initiation, the sun and the moon.

This all evolved more than 500 years ago and was based on even more ancient Greek and Egyptian knowledge as well as, probably, others. Certainly, the science of genetic engineering and the cloning of the perfect human being has preoccupied man for a very long time, and probably since he first stood up and took a look at himself in the murky water's reflection from which he had just emerged.

Equally, the search for the perfect drink has always been of fundamental curiosity and had a far deeper resonance with human existence than the mere slaking of the thirst.

The secret power of the alembic lies in the fact that it does so relate to the form of a beautiful woman and, therefore, must also be the producer of the miracles of life, its abundance, sensuous promise and aromatic dreams. As well as being the producer, the alembic is also referred to as the Receiver. It is all things to all men.

Earliest Western European pot-still production. Salerno, Italy, AD 1480, or Strasbourg, AD 1590, if you believe another source. However, I reckon it was Abergele, North Wales, AD 1329, – cow-dung molasses, or whisky boyo, in Celtic slang.

The Welsh have been seriously overlooked in the history of whisky-making, when, in fact, it was they who first fermented the lanolin, secreted in sheep's wool, and distilled it into a warrior's battle-cry and a Druid's tonic. Its long-term effects, however, were disastrous and made the Welsh easy prey to the English, in spite of the fervent and inspirational leadership of Owen Glyndwr.

But all this was, of course, faithfully recorded in the Boyo Tapestry, which was, unfortunately, chewed to bits by Gwenellen's goat. Only a remnant remains and today it looks like nothing more than a ragged old rugby scarf.

In the picture, the still operators are wearing Welsh tartan. But, I digress.

Wysg (WELSH = a stream). The Welsh, too, distilled everything they could get there hands on. In an attempt to distil the very knowledge of the Druids, they boiled their books and distilled the resulting fermented mash. It drove sane men mad and wise men idiotic. The cause was traced to a particular kind of book glue used at the time, the boilings of the bones of the now extinct Welsh Elephant Bird imported from Madagascar and used by the Druids to ride in state to the great stone of Llanfairfechan for the Solstice ceremony. Today the Welsh make their own whisky or Wysg and so they should . . .

COSMIC FURNACE

Left: A cosmic furnace evolved in the madness of the dark, in which sulphur, salt and mercury would unite to create the Philosopher's Stone, the conjunction of the male and female principles.

Scottish alchemists abounded in the Middle Ages, all trying desperately to turn haggis into gold. Their endeavours resulted in the cosmic furnace which transformed barley, wheat and oats into porridge. This lumpy, grey dish suited the easily satisfied Scots' palate for centuries until it was discovered that the addition of salt made the mix even more unsavoury, thus ensuring the continued relish with which the Scots revere their national dish.

Phoenicians (1500–332 BC) were sea traders depending for their wealth on their access to the Mediterranean along the coast of Syria and Mount Lebanon, the land of Canaan in the Bible. They believed that the Greeks based their mythology on them. Their name came from Phoenix, the son of the first King of Agenor. The wines of dates and grapes are quoted as being the offerings to the gods, who were expected to need nourishment like mortals: Come give them drink. Put bread upon the table and pour wine into the cups. IN THE GOLDEN GOBLET THE BLOOD OF TREES. Give unto them the essence of sacrifice, the pure vapours of fruit, that they may dwell happily in the world of spirits. Presiding over all things was troubled and windy air or a breath of wind and dark chaos which became enamoured of itself, fused with itself, and called this union desire. This was believed to be the creation of the world, made up of all decomposed rot and slime of aquatic substance. It is an evocative description of the nature of fermentation and distillation.

Meanwhile Druids manipulated the populace of Celtic madness in the dark recesses of history, seeking solace in potions of weird and dangerous uncertainty. Willing volunteers, spurred on by threats of physical damage and eternal damnation in an even darker state of misery, became the tasters of these eclectic brews and distillations. The Druids measured the mortality rate of these luckless individuals, who knew life only on the receiving end of thrashings and bitter experience brought on by an accident of birth. The Druids claimed each new death to be a scientific breakthrough.

When the dark ages descended on man, the Celts had already decamped west from Asia. Probably originating from a race of people of schizoid paranoic spirit, one half of the race split and went south-east from Indo-China, in the days when there was still land mass from Java to Darwin in Northern Australia.

The remainder were a devious and errant bunch of rampaging originals who left their

mark across Asia, Eastern and Western Europe and the Isles of Britain. Remains of their weapons of stone and bronze have been found across the whole surface of the earth, save the Polynesian Archipelago, and have become known as Thunderbolts or Thunder Weapons. The Celts looked west for their destiny and still do. They have moved west since the dawn of time, and it is they who will ultimately discover the meaning of life by disappearing up themselves, as is the nature of all Celts.

By coracle, to Islay from Ireland, they came, bringing their filthy habits with them, and their wives and children.

Islay is a mere 17 miles from the coast of Ireland and, on arrival on this offshore piece of Argyll in the 6th century AD, the Brythonic Celts established a new territory which they called Dalriada. They defended it furiously, keeping at bay the many Pictish tribes who roamed the north-western areas of Britain, which was then called Alba. The Celts had brought with them their particularly Celtic form of speech, and after many battles on Jura and Gigha, during the 7th and 8th centuries, they reluctantly united with the Picts.

The Scots' language was adopted largely through hand-to-hand exchanges like 'Ow! Gerraff! Yur breakin' ma airm!!' or 'Heh! Get yur knee aff ma 'neck!! I cannae breathe!!'

It was likely that some form of crude distillation occurred and any doubting Pict was probably won over with a wee dram of fermented gruts. Porridge was and still is the opium of the people.

*Friar Cor, according to
the Exchequer Rolls of
1494, accepting eight
bolls of malt for the
making of aqua vitae.*

WHISKERY

Six hundred years later, the art of distillation is believed to have been carried over the waters, a mere 17 miles, to Islay, where an abundance of peat, pure soft water and fertile soil provided all that was necessary to make Islay the perfect kingdom for the development of the national drink of Scotland – *Uisge Beatha.*

The Hebrides came under Norwegian rule, and King Haco took an expedition south in 1263, in an attempt to maintain sovereignty over all the islands. He just could not figure out what it was that drove the island Scots frantic and made them such a formidable fighting force. Being Uisge Beathe'd up to the eyeballs, the islanders simply knew no fear.

Robert Bruce (AD 1274–1329) was the one who secured independence for Scotland. He was crowned at Scone in 1306, as Robert I, and set about reclaiming Scottish towns and castles in English possession. He whipped the English at Bannockburn, in 1314, by following the example of a spider who tried and tried until he reached the top of a rope in a cave hideout Bruce was sharing with him at the time. That part of the legend is believed to be apochryphal, but it is acknowledged by Scottish historians, that, considering the fact that the Scots invented everything else, it was then that Robert Bruce probably invented the teabag, before going into battle.

John Knox led the Protestant Reformation in Scotland in the 16th century and the Scots were now Calvinists with a powerful drink on their hands. It was this combination, this struggle between puritan restraint and native appetite for their national drink, that created what I think became the characteristic dark soul of whisky.

The whisky began to moofle gloriously, making clans fight like fury over the rights to fresh running mountain burns for the making of it. There were no distilleries as business establishments at the time, since everybody made their own. The English had not yet begun to realise the revenue that the drink could generate. Throughout the 16th century these clans, both warring and friendly, lived in a world of their own, oblivious to the intentions and plans of the Scottish Crown. They plundered and raped and pillaged because it was profitable and therefore a good idea.

Distilling was now firmly established. It used a coarse brew of local cereals (oats). Destructive in its effect, this water of life might have put whiskers on the back of a great warrior, but it probably left the tender hearted writhing in agony.

The Isles, however, remained lawless. Criminals and smugglers lived there like lords of a twilight world. The Stewart succession to the English throne exacerbated James VI's efforts to settle the 'Isles problem'. The Royal Court was moved to London in March 1603, and James VI attempted to create a united Britain, a perfect union of laws and people all under the one umbrella ruler – him. Desperate for total control he attempted a policy of genocide against the islanders in 1607. The Marquess of Huntly was to be the execu-

tioner. The Presbyterians on the Privy Council objected to this Catholic having all the fun and the plan was aborted with the confinement of the Marquess in Elgin. Drink was cited as one of the prime reasons why the islanders were so unruly.

A social statute was set up at Iona in a vain attempt to bring the island chiefs into line, forbidding their primitive ways. The Kirk had to be attended, inns were set up for proper regulation of victuals. Malingerers could no longer use the excuse of being employed as some kind of minder to chiefs. Beggars were outlawed and chiefs could no longer mete out vicious punishment just for fun whilst under the influence of strong drink. Smuggling had to stop and in recompense all islanders were allowed to distil their own liquor for their own households, and only the gentry could order other kinds of alcoholic beverage from the mainland. The first son of the gentry had to go to the mainland to learn English; or a daughter, if the son was too drunk. Firearms were forbidden and travelling bards were banned as carriers of dangerous ideas amongst the populace.

The Union of Parliaments in 1707 created the greatest smouldering resentment between a Scotland all but disinherited, and a disinterested Westminster, which, whilst leaving Scotland to its own internal devices, imposed impractical taxes in an attempt to stem rampant illicit distilling. The Malt Tax of 1713 was one of the most erratic. As an appeasing gesture, the Government halved the tax on malted barley in Scotland, but this only led to an increase in the illegal stills at work, and a far superior malt whisky than that produced by those legal stills paying twice as much for their barley, who, therefore cut their supplies with inferior raw grain.

It was the task of a new breed of revenue officers from England to enforce these taxation laws but their job was made virtually impossible, since the regions of the most intense illicit acitivity, the Highlands, were impregnable in any practical way. Much stumbling, cursing and even shirking was the result.

A frenzy of differently styled taxation followed before and after the Battle of Culloden

in 1746. Resentment continued to mount, riots, intrigue and smuggling intensified.

General Wade, a loyal Hanoverian soldier who was more of an engineer than a fighting man, recommended that forts, barracks and particularly roads and bridges be built to create access for the British army and allow them, thereby, to control the Highlands. He was despatched to build roads through the Highlands and soldiers were garrisoned at Inverness, Fort William, Crieff, Fort Augustus and Fort George, engaged in the hopeless task of controlling the rebellious Jacobites, confiscating their weapons and supporting the revenue officers. Over a period of seven years, from 1726 to 1733, Wade built 260 miles of roads, and during the next 4 years, nearly 40 bridges. The road building went on after Wade and, following initial resentment, became popular as a convenience to all those

who needed to move quickly. It served the Jacobites just as well as their oppressors.

A 1786 Distillery Act applied an extra tax on the whole of Scottish production of still spirit and another tax on spirit imported into England. Nothing, however, could stop the illicit trade which probably reached gargantuan proportions at this time. Smuggling was a long-term career and whisky flowed south like a tidal wave.

Westminster pursued a vindictive course against the Highlanders, 'loyal' and 'disloyal' alike. The really harsh measure was a ban on the small stills, followed by frequent increases in duty on whisky, as demand for whisky grew in England. In defiance and amidst riots, even more private illicit stills sprang up everywhere, and Burns' *Freedom and Whisky gang thegither* became a kind of battle cry. Armies of gaugers with military support were let loose, but the illicit stills thrived in every farm and in every wash house and anywhere unobtrusive enough to secrete a sma' still.

It was an heroic age, a battle of wills and cunning between the hunted smugglers and the desperate and hated gaugers in pursuit. These activities created their own traditional pedigree of rich folklore. The heroes were the hunted, and the villains were a jealous Hanoverian government out to suppress the last relic of an ancient Gaelic civilisation. The 1814 Act, which declared a capacity of 500 gallons to be the smallest still legally permitted, effectively outlawed every distiller in Scotland, and there was then a new ruling following an 1823 Royal Commission's findings. This resulted in lower duty of 2 shillings and 3 pence per gallon of proof spirit, and a new licence fee of 40 pounds for stills over 40 gallons capacity. Anything smaller was obviously for illicit dealing and as a law it was in its way rather cunning. It is difficult to nip about in the heather with anything larger – but even that did not stop them. (Try running to catch a bus carrying a bucket of water – and that's just two gallons.) It is practically impossible to snuff out a whole way of life through mere legislation. The government had to learn to work with and not against society and what it saw as its inalienable rights.

Boswell and Johnson took the high road when they left Aberdeen for Skye via Elgin, Inverness, down along the western shores of Loch Ness to Invermoriston and through to Glenelg. Here they were guided by a manservant after having spent a night on a bed of hay but with no hospitality. The manservant returned as they waited to cross to Skye with a present of rum and sugar to warm their insides. On the return journey, they stopped at Inverary, where Boswell records that Dr Johnson, who had not touched a drop of fermented liquor throughout the whole journey (apart, one supposes, from the rum), asked for a gill of whisky 'to find out what it is that makes a Scottishman happy'. He drank the lot, save for a dribble which Boswell tasted, so that Boswell could say that they had drunk whisky together.

Highland Bull

Ralph Steadman '83

MONARCH of the GLEN

Labels on map: HEBRIDES, SKYE, TALISKER, HIGHLANDS, SPEYSIDE, PULTENEY, CLYNELISH, DINGWALL, INVERNESS, BOTHVELL AND JOHNSON, CULLODEN, GLEN GARIOCH, ABERDEEN, DALWHINNIE, PERTH, THE BORDER, DUNDEE, OBAN, MULL, JURA, ISLAY, ARRAN, CAMPBELLTOWN, SPRINGBANK, Mull of KINTYRE, EDINBURGH, GLASGOW, GLEN KINCHIE, LOWLANDS, NOTHING, BLADNOCH, CARLISLE, N

Islay

Islay malts are known particularly for their peatiness, and a strong salt-sprayed, aye, aye, Cap'n, seaweedy flavour; they are the most pungent of all whiskies. Islay remains a self-contained powerhouse of distinction and I will eulogise upon the subject strictly on request.

The REGIONS

Campbeltown

Campbeltown is on a large substantial peninsula, enclosing the Isle of Arran and protecting it in a way that suggests something rather manly and virile. It is no accident that the church bell in Campbeltown is blessed with a loud dong. There is nothing camp about that bell. The pun is irresistible and so is the whisky – strong-bodied, pulsating warmth and a salty tang of smugglers' caves. Nowadays, only two distilleries, Glen Scotia and Springbank, are in action out of the 33 that flourished in the vaporous days of mid-19th century optimism. By the time Alfred Barnard visited, in 1885, 20 were going strong and they continued to do so until World War I. Some were mothballed, then reopened, only to be withered by American Prohibition in the 1920s.

Lowlands

Lowland whiskies are lighter, with a sweeter quality. But some, like Auchentoshan, are triple-distilled, light, but intense and nutty, rather like one of those geldings in fettle again! They get leaner and less sweet with age, but who doesn't? For a whisky, it is a bonus.

Highlands

Highland malts are the spoiled brats of whiskies, which only means that they have got it all – eagles, red deer, grouse, heather moors, lochs, glens, mountain peaks and wildest abandon.

Smoky, rather than peaty, they exude a kind of Scottish pride and wealth, which is considered sophisticated. In many ways it is, but, to an outsider, it can also be interpreted as an over-exercised national pride and smugness which, thankfully, are absent from the Highlands' superlative art of whisky-making. The Highlanders are generous and ingenious enough to make sure that only that which is breathtaking and lifegiving about their environment is put inside a handy bottle, with a hint of sweetness to help it on its way to softening the stoniest heart. (My editor is a Scotsman, and he appreciates the poetic bits.)

The Speyside single malts, along the river Spey, are especially favoured by blenders to balance their blends because of the sublety of the style. Nothing is too pronounced, except the concentration of fine distilleries in this region. Further east there is a thinning-out of distilleries and a more varied style and quality which perhaps discourages all but the most daring blenders, bearing in mind that consistency is the yardstick and even a restraining conservatism – but that is only my triple-distilled opinion.

Orkney

The Orkney Islands are a Nordic law unto themselves, and the stronghold of one of the finest malts it has ever been my privilege to watch in production and to taste in profusion – Highland Park.

CULLODEN

A visit to Inverness, to attend the 1993 Cartoon Forum, left us with a whole Saturday with nothing to do. A whole Saturday ahead with vast vistas of loch-side slopes and rolling heather glens beckoning. The call of the wild and a clutch of distilleries is a strong incentive. We needed a car.

The Hotel Caledonian doesn't seem to understand the concept of car travel and gave us an Avis rental number. We rang them and they wanted £80 a day and the car was at the airport, ten miles out of town. All the rest, Hertz, Europcar, Budget, etc were booked up and we felt stranded. The Tourist Office, however, gave us a whole list of local people and one by one we picked them off – all busy, except one – Sharp's Reliable Wrecks. They had a perfect little Fiat Uno, a pleasant manner, and an unbelievably cheap day rate.

We tried to find the A9 and missed it, but drove instead into the Culloden Battlefield. There was blood everywhere, red and yellow flags flying, souvenirs, people struggling and kicking to get to the check-out desk, and guided tours every 20 minutes to explain why Culloden is Scotland's patent and indelible reason for hating the English.

The Duke of Cumberland, aptly known as 'the Butcher', a fat slob of English respectability and pink offal, stood wax-still at the entrance, sporting a mere half of his actual real life girth (a fire precaution). He is famous for routing the Jacobite troops of Bonnie Prince Charlie and then setting about one of the most hideous post-battle slaughters in history, hacking to death many men, women and children as they fled to high ground. Some were only bystanders, idle gawpers with a mawkish interest in anything out of the ordinary, covered in blood and gore, and who are usually referred to by historians as the 'innocent'.

The battleground is a rough, pot-holed heather-strewn plot of ground, completely unsuited to the Highlanders' fighting techniques, which involved lots of sword brandishing, shouting and sprinting forward with malicious intent, not to mention kiltless. But an all-night march on the 15th April 1746 had left them tired, demoralised and ill-equipped. Sleet swept straight into their raw red faces as they faced the enemy. Bonnie Prince Charlie had been badly advised.

The Government troops, however, were well-equipped, fresh and ready to rout the rebels without mercy. Grapeshot, a vicious conglomerate of any bits of iron, nails, lead, jammed down the nose of a cannon, ripped holes through the Jacobite lines in minutes and the battle was all over in an hour with over 1,200 Jacobites dead and the rest slaughtered where they stood, or hunted like animals for sport.

It was probably this event more than any other which set the attitude of the Scots towards the English for the next two centuries. With the imposition of the spiteful Malt Tax in 1812, it became a matter of honour for the Scots to avoid paying for anything by any means at their disposal, for any reason. Ironically, this very attitude may be the source of the image the Scots have worldwide for being as mean as the English are stiff and reserved. In fact, the Scots are careful but generous, and the English *are* stiff and reserved.

After several inspired guesses we found a route which appeared to go in the direction of the distilleries to the north of Inverness, but instead took us in a south-westerly direction, down along the banks of Loch Ness.

It was perfect. The day was balmy and the view breathtaking. White sails were dotted around for miles and there was no hint of mists or dark, gloomy waters. It was only when I decided to paddle in the clear waters lapping gently on the peat-blown stones that the sky turned black, a wind swept through the length of the waters and the shape of some prehistoric alembic monolith reared up, casting pleasure boats aside like matchwood.

I stepped back out of the water in horror and, immediately, the scene was as peaceful and idyllic as before. I stepped forward once more, put my toe in, and again the sky turned black, the winds blew and the copper-black madness reared up in front of me. I recoiled again and everything was sheer magnificence and calm.

Meanwhile, Anna was quietly filling in her diary, completely unaware of my experience and the terrifying sight.

'I think it's time we moved on,' she said gently.

'I have just seen the Loch Ness Monster,' I declared. 'It's on the rampage!'

Unconcerned, she gathered up her things and I followed her as she muttered something about finding a little pub somewhere for a spot of lunch.

next page!

The STILL of LOCH NESS

Ralph STEADman

GLEN TURRET

Ralph (speaking into tape recorder): I'm up above the distillery of Glenturret, looking round at the most wonderful vist – aaaaaarrrggghhhh!!! shit!!! and I'm surrounded by oh bugger it, it's all over my shoes, rabbit warrens and hundreds of rabbits all dropping everyth – sod it! – running about all over the place – my foot! I can't move my foot!! John call the emergenc – what? can't hear – goddamnit – never mind – aaaarrrrrggggghhhh!!!! OK – clambering out – moving to different places as I move along and I'm on a sort of slopeaaaarrrgggghhh, shit, sod it, a little bit dodgy but otherwise it's all right – OK, no problem

I can unfortunately only see the Pagoda Restaurant – bloody awful food – what can you expect from Scaaaarrrggghhhtish barbarians – raaaaarrrrggggghhhh!! liver? – I can't quite see round the corner to the old distillery itself. There it is! Yes!! – and there's one of the buildings still here – there – which has been turned into a baaaarrrgggggghhhhh!!! and restaurant heaving with tourism. But I can hear the river from here. I can just see it amongst the trees, a beautiful brown waaaaarrrggghhhhhttteeerrr, shit!, clear as a bell – but with that tinge of brown, a peaty – look out!! . . . foot!!! damn the sodding

Loch Turret Dam. Ralph Steadman

rabbits!! the water of the Turret River. I can just gaaaaarrrr – aaaarrrrggggghhhh!! the sheer beauty of this location, one of the most beautiful locations aaarrrgggggve! seen for a distillery and it is the oldest distillery, 1775 an' all that, closed down 1921 during prohibition and arrrgghhhhh!!-fter a heavy war. Re-opened in 1959 as an independent distillery. Now it belongs to Matthew Glaaaarrrggghhhagg!! – and I have to say that they aaarrrggggghhhh seem to be involved with Matthew Gloag – I just said that – my foot!! aarrggghhh!!!! – can't keep their hands off aaaaaarrrggghhhhh!!! – who can these days – what th – ! sod these badgers! – it's badgers!! – it isn't rabbits at all. Bloody badgers!!! – they're a menace to civilised whisky distillery observers nationwide – and this is Angus Macaaaarrggghhh-ity returning you to the – no wait a minute! – there appear to be several badger sets around here, large holes, or they may be fox holes or old bothy holes. They are holes. Yes, I can tell you at this moment in time that they are holes. I'm making my way down now. The leaves are too full to quite see the rooftops of the distillery. There's the water tank and I've got to get down behind that – aaarrrggghhhh!!!!!!! there's a path down. Shit! That's another hole . . . at this point I seem to have switched off my tape recorder or something . . . shit!!!

Almost a mile away above the Glen is the new dam holding back the clear water of Loch Turret. Its pristine newness contrasts strangely with the rugged magnificent mountain ranges which rise majestically along its banks. The dam wall projects its own kind of odd comparison and the mind boggles at the millions of gallons of potential whisky held there in suspended animation. What a booze-up!

I'm not sure about Glenturret. It has everything in its favour and yet it only tells us that. It never really understands its pedigree or declares it nonchalantly – which I think, it should. It clasps desperately at the arm of a passer-by. It searches out a baleful gaze and screeches – guess what? We are the oldest distillery in Scotland!! 'Aw gee, that's really sometun! I'm an American, not the oldest, but it sure is great to meet the oldest. I'm the oldest in Nebraska, mind, but I ain't dead yet. I bin there 34 years! Can you beat that? Huh – 276 years old, eh. Wowee! This is an old place, Yessir! You bin doing Bourbon a long time. Goddamn! That's near 150 years older than Jack Daniels himself. Boy, could that man make whisky. I never knew a whisky like Jack's.'

It is a great single malt and it doesn't deserve such banter, even in jest. The area was alive with illicit bothies in the heroic times. The site upon which Glenturret stands most certainly was such a place – probably the prime site, well entrenched in a steep-sided Glen and awash with moofling and the collecting of precious liquids. The water from the burn is just running – pure, soft, fresh and cold. Full of the properties that make Scotland the most ideal situation for the most balanced magic in the world.

Two high hills on either side of the site

afforded excellent look-out places for smugglers' mates. No old print I have seen does its snug location justice and today it still retains that feeling of secretive isolation. Coming along from the nearest small town of Crieff you could miss it on the bend as you approach.

Found on a wall along the River Tay:

The average Englishman in a home he calls his castle, slips into his national costume, a shabby raincoat, patented by chemist, Charles Mackintosh from Glasgow, Scotland. En route to his office he strides along the English lane surfaced by John Macadam of Ayr, Scotland. He drives an English car fitted with tyres invented by John Boyd Dunlop of Dreghorn, Scotland. At the office he receives the mail, bearing adhesive stamps invented by John Chalmers of Dundee, Scotland. During the day he uses the telephone, invented by Alexander Graham Bell, born in Edinburgh, Scotland. At home in the evening his daughter peddles her bicycle invented by Kirpatrick Macmillan Smith of Dumfries, Scotland. He watches the news on TV, an invention of John Baird of Helensburgh, Scotland. And here's an item about the US Navy founded by John Paul Jones of Kirkbeen, Scotland. He had now been reminded too much of Scotland and in desperation he picked up the Bible only to find that the first man mentioned in the good book is a Scot, King James VI, who authorised its translation. Nowhere can an Englishman turn to escape the ingenuity of the Scots. He could take a drink. The Scots make the best in the world. He could take a rifle and end it all, but the breach-loading rifle was invented by Captain Patrick Ferguson of Pitfours, Scotland. If he escaped death he could find himself on an operating table injected with penicillin discovered by Alexander Fleming of Darvel, Scotland, given an anaesthetic, discovered by Sir James Young Simpson of Bathgate, Scotland. Out of the anaesthetic he would find no comfort in learning that he was as safe as the Bank of England, founded by William Paterson of Dumfries, Scotland. Perhaps his only remaining hope is to get a transfusion of good Scottish blood which would entitle him to ask, 'Wha's like us? Nemo me impune lacessit.' Even chauvinism was invented by the Scots but they are far too modest to mention that.

Old Meldrum landscape, Aberdeenshire

Royal BRACKLA

A distillery I had never heard of, but which now stands out in my mind as a particularly distinctive one.

Standing inside the still room, which houses four stills, I looked out at what is perhaps the most convenient juxtaposition I have ever seen. To my left, are the old bonded warehouses. Centrally placed are the three reservoirs constantly refilled by the Cawdor Burn, where all the water for distilling Royal Brackla is drawn. There is an underground water supply, which is now used exclusively to cool the swirling spirit vapours which rise like Palamino horses from the stills. To my right, and immediately alongside Cawdor Burn Reservoir, is the barley field. What immaculate planning!

Unfortunately, this rare single malt is only available at the distillery itself, or from selected distributors in the Lowlands. This was a tradition started by the founder, Captain William Fraser of Brackla House. He became a licensed distiller, early in the 19th century, but found it very difficult to compete with the illicit stills, who paid nothing to nobody and didn't intend to. This did not seem fair to him and he reported his plight to a Parliamentary Commission in 1821. He had sold less than 100 gallons for immediate consumption within a radius of 120 miles in a year, and yet, inhabitants for miles around drank whisky, and only whisky, like Coca Cola.

Hence the development of a distribution network in the Lowlands and an advertising campaign, plus King William IV's blessing. He commanded a regular supply at his royal chambers from 1835, in the thieving tradition of royal personages.

It seems that between 1827 and 1844 Captain Fraser got into a spot of trouble with H.M. Customs and Excise. I suspect that His Majesty became a useful ally at that time and, in exchange for overlooking certain discrepancies, earned the Captain's devotion.

It became known as 'The King's Own Whisky' and Captain Fraser mended his ways. Hence the prefix 'Royal' to the name Brackla.

Royal BRACKLA Distillery — THE VIEW.

Royal Brackla prospered with the blessing of the new Excise Act of 1823, which eased restrictions on those who went legal. It earned the title 'The Drink Divine', and Queen Victoria gave it a Royal Warrant of Appointment in 1838.

The House of Andrew Usher & Co. of Edinburgh became Royal Brackla's agents until the turn of the century. It was the Ushers who introduced the art of blending in the 1860s and, together with the Frasers, created proprietary blends, probably some of the first of their kind offered to the public.

Brackla was the stiff drink favoured by explorers seeking the source of the Nile in the 1860s and is eulogised in diaries and letters of the period. 'My dear Fanny, I am bearing up. The river is longer than I imagined. The tigers can be a trifle bothersome but I bag them when I can. The worst are the mosquitoes which can only be held at bay when my blood is pulsating with a goodly snort of Brackla'.

All the distilleries of Islay are built next to the sea. In the old days when the small ships had to come in, there was no point in having a distillery ten miles inland. It had to get to Scotland. On a really stormy day, the sea's over that wall. That gate we just drove in, I've seen barrels floating out that gate. Empty ones!

Jim McEwan, Bowmore distillery

Caol ILA Distillery
with MARINE PANORAMA
ISLAY.

PEAT

Cutting peat is perhaps one of the less common pursuits of ordinary folk and, I would imagine, is practically non-existent among the aristocracy, though I heard a whisper that the occasional Irish lord would take his turn, between hangovers, to clear the head. Peat bogs are invariably windswept and, in that way, perfectly situated for the purpose for which they were cut, which was generally to keep a body warm. Basically, peat is cut as a fuel which, being dense in texture in its waterlogged state, is extracted from straight-cut peat-banks and left to dry in long 18 inch by 5 inch square blocks in wigwam-style piles called fixings. When dry, it is black and hard and, in some cases, not unlike coal.

Cutting peat is not an unpleasant experi-ence, if you only have a yard or so to deal with. If you are a serious peat cutter with a real purpose then you purchase about 80 yards of peat bog, about a yard wide, and you cut 18 inch-deep furrows. First, cut off the top 8 inches of grass-covered peat before removing your particular area. This amount will keep a fire going for an average heavy Scottish winter, and fill your house with the most delicious, aromatic and musty smell you can imagine.

The tools used to cut this fuel supply con-

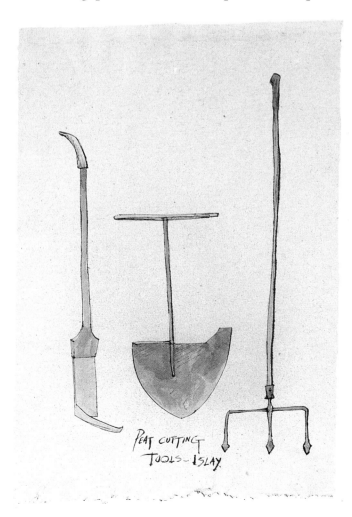

PEAT CUTTING
TOOLS—ISLAY

PEAT
CUTTERS and
GOLDEN EAGLE

sist of a flat shovel to remove the top layer; then a right-angled cutting tool with a cranked horn-bone handle on the holding-end, to control the direction of the cut. This enables you to cut directly downwards, but at a slight angle, so that the soft cheeselike piece can be lifted out all within the same motion and laid on the grass-covered bank at your side. The third tool is a three-pronged fork for lifting out fallen pieces, whole or broken, to be laid neatly side-by-side with the rest. A peatcutter refreshes his parts with a mixture of water and oats – uncooked porridge in fact. It quenches your thirst like nothing else.

Deeper channels are cut periodically, to allow water to drain away, particularly from areas where you are working, otherwise flooding would result and work would be impossible. Attention is given to the depth of cut in one area to control the overall regularity so that, at a later date, another layer can be extracted with as much ease and uniformity as the cut before.

There is also a machine for peat cutting

which is regrettably rather like open cast mining. An area is literally chain-sawed out by a 4-inch wide chain saw of scoops which drives the peat into a compressor and out through a series of fanned tubes like spaghetti. These are allowed to dry in the sun and wind before being collected by a harvester conveyor-belt which throws the turd-shaped pieces into a truck moving alongside the tractor. All vehicles have at least three tyres per wheel to minimise the sinking of the heavy machinery into the sponge-like peat which reacts like a waterbed underfoot.

When you cut three feet down with a peat chain saw and gouge out the under matter, what fills it up? Is it water? Does it create a waterlogged substrata? Professor Brad Quatako of Ottawa Institute of Advanced Peataqua Studies at the University of Algonquin says, 'Yes, and worse, air too, which turns foul when trapped. It causes embarrassing histrionic effects when trodden on. It could mean the end of romance for the peat dwellers.'

I suspect that with continuous moving pressure of this intensity, the time-formed nature of the oily substance breaks down and its inherent qualities are impaired, if not damaged forever.

How environmentally friendly this mechanised invasion is will only be revealed in time. It is the subject of much debate, and various pressure groups have voiced many objections to its practice, particularly against its use in the malting of barley where it is burned in furnaces topped by pagoda-shaped drying attics. It is this drying and smoking process which imparts to whisky, especially Islay whisky, its seaweedy pungent flavour, the 'medicinal' characteristic of Islay single malts. Two thirds of the burning goes up in CO_2 – but oxygen is created. Nothing is wasted, I can vouch for that, and whisky distilling is still one of the most effectively environmentally friendly industries. Even the boiled barley mash is recycled as cattle fodder called draff.

It seemed like a good idea at the time, but nothing is replaced. Peat cannot be replaced

Ralph Steadman. Derelict Croft & Peat Furrows, Islay – 2 Sept 91.

In those days the men used to get five or six drams and the old boys preferred it straight from the still – white spirit. In the summer time we had a problem because there was no white spirit being produced, so the manager would say to me, 'Go and draw us a really good dram for the lads at five o'clock. Choose the best dram.' The really old worthies would come in and say it wasn't strong enough! They liked a really good hit. It all stopped in 1978.

Jim McEwan, Bowmore distillery

Below: Machined peat

any more than coal can. The increased demand for the raw material of the land imposes a pressure that had never existed before. The industrialised peat cutting can only disturb an environmental balance that was maintained in earlier times. The local needs were in rhythm with the available resources. The peat was cut for basic heating and a much smaller whisky output. The top soil was replaced and the land resumed its natural course. Its wildlife was hardly damaged, merely disturbed temporarily. Now vast tracts of peat bog lie like open wounds, and the mechanical disturbance, even the massive weight of its bulk, compressing the ground in such an unprecedented fashion, is reminiscent of the despoliation of forests to make way for new roads – a despoliation from which the land never recovers. No one can really say whether such policies are good or bad ones, since they have never been tried before. Mechanical peat cutting appears to show the same propensity for damage, as other forms of exploitation, in other industries. While it may certainly be easier on the back, and a machine can do the work of a hundred men in a fraction of the time, what price the future if unseen cycles of nature's regenerative forces cause other bio-systems to live or die?

GlenRothes Distillery - Speyside

GLENROTHES DISTILLERY CATHEDRAL, Speyside.

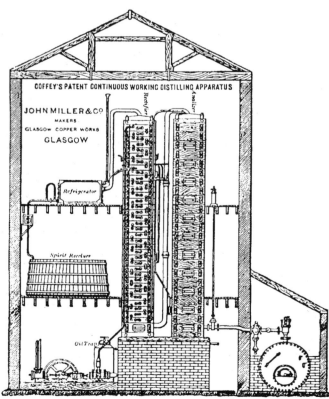

Above: Forsythe's Still-yard, Rothes

Ralph STEADman 9/3

Patent STILL

The patent still revolutionised whisky-making. It was originally invented by Richard Stein, in 1826, but was perfected by Aeneas Coffey in the 1850s which has established him as its inventor. Grain was used in a continuous process which speeded up the production of basic industrial spirit and hastened in the science of blending various distilled liquors with pure single malts from the various regions of Scotland. Independent of geographic location, it created an outrage and to some became a mockery of the traditional drink familiar to Scotsmen everywhere. It seemed to strike at the very heart of stills of illicit magnificence.

Copper Stills and Mash

It has to be copper – only copper will do. Copper is soft and copper is clean – come and get me, copper! A cut from copper will heal about a week earlier than it does if you cut yourself on steel. Try it. Copper is beaten and steel is rolled, and copper is fashioned by machine into more regular shapes like mash-tuns, washbacks and fermentation tanks with straight sides.

Coppersmiths always made pot stills by hand. They had to and they still do, but they do other things to survive in our rapidly changing world of virtual reality. Rarely does a new distillery open, and those in existence require a new still but it is only a once-in-a-lifetime occurrence. But stills do need repairs. Some parts of a still wear out quicker than others, so repair work is a fairly constant necessity. A visit to Forsyth's in Rothes is a visit to a metalwork factory of great diversity.

The heads and swan necks of a pot still go first, after about 10 to 12 years, because of the corrosive effect of the low wine vapours (the first distillation) on the metal. The bulging part, the pot, will last 20 to 25 years, maybe more. Then the bottom will go on a direct-fire still, where the heat, at anything between 600 and 700 degrees centigrade, is in direct contact with the thicker copper bottom. The indirectly heated pot stills have thinner copper bottoms, but will last longer. They have an internal, tubular, stainless steel heating ring, rather like an electric kettle, with added fancy cylindrical augmenters to increase the heating surface and distribute the heat more efficiently inside the pot. Condensers, the cooling part of the distillation process, will last about 25 years, but they too may develop faults at different times in their labyrinth of copper tubing, inside the main cold water trunk, which is also made of copper.

Ancient Stills, Strathisla
(Heart of Chivas Regal) (circa 1786)

All that has changed over 200-odd years are the welding techniques, but the joints are still hand-hammered into shape. Because they taper and curve in so many directions, each section will be made from three or four smaller sections.

Some pot stills have a swelling at the base of the neck like a huge goiter, called a boil-ball, or Ogee in Greek, which is meant to compensate for reflux. Reflux is the fallback of vapours which don't quite make it over the top of the swan neck and condense backwards, as it were. Reflux is corrosive. In attempts to minimise this effect, necks have been widened, narrowed, squatted, heightened, and boilballed, but the essential alembic shape has never changed. The slight differences and sizes have all evolved out of hunches, constant performance results, habits, and, probably, accidents. Beliefs in some inherent and mystical ability proven by results over generations are peculiar to any and every distillery, including superstition, and dents in the copper that may well be the very thing that singles out one malt from another. The dents are always replaced exactly as they were whenever repairs are made.

Denters, of course, are artists and command great respect and humbling. You can't just make any old dent with a big hammer and walk away. It requires the ear and intuition of a piano tuner to hit the right note, and, if it's not right, a whole panel may have to be made again, at great cost. It could be claimed that a fractional mistake could mar the whole symphony, which after all is what the whisky-making process is. Likewise, you cannot learn denting; you are born with it. Many Scottish households encourage their offspring, hardly out of nappies, by giving them hammers and the kitchen pots and pans, to bang away to their hearts' content in the hope of discovering a born denter in the family. Those who haven't quite got the knack often become drummers in the Argyll Highlanders. But I digress . . .

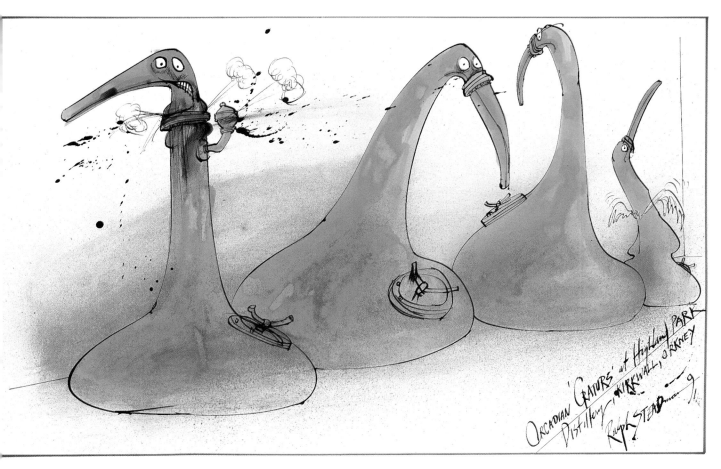

'Orcadian Craturs' at Highland Park Distillery, Kirkwall, Orkney — Ralph Steadman

Glen Ord

Glen Ord has many parts of its 19th-century architecture intact, although the bonded warehouses are renovated. The newer additions sit awkwardly, as though a part of something else. The pot stills stand proudly, however – a row of six copper icons, glowing in the sunlight shining through the window-fronted facade.

That is its most spectacular feature. The rest is functional, bleak and corrugated. Glen Ord's own maltings are colossal, the tallest in Scotland, and dominate the surrounding flat countryside for miles.

COOPERAGE

There was a cooper and his cask, with a hey and a ho and a hey nonny no! . . .

Speyside is the heart of the Scottish malt whisky industry, if only because more of it is produced in this area and with more consistency over a longer period.

It is also central, geographically, and is therefore surrounded by all the rest, even

FIRING A CASK — SPEYSIDE COOPERAGE.

Donny's Inferno
In firing an old cask, the heads are removed from each end and it is placed over a furnace, with a metal plate laid over the top. The heat builds up inside and the wood is, quite literally, toasted. Then the cooper removes the metal plate, allowing the intense heat to burst out. It is removed from the heat and hosed until it is cool. This process restores the toasty flavours to the wood and over the years, these influence the nature of the whisky. Casks are blistered in the firing and this roughness is left to add to the flavour-imparting properties of the oak. The flames sterilise every tiny crack. Nothing purifies like fire, except whisky itself.

CROSS SECTION OF TREE SHOWING HOW THE BULK IS PLANKED — THE RINGS SHOULD CROSS THE PLANK AS DIRECTLY AS POSSIBLE TO MINIMISE WARPING.

THE COOPER'S WOOD AND TOOLS

CHIME

HEAD

QUARTER

BOOGE

PITCH

BOOGE

QUARTER

CHIME

BOW SAW

DRESSED STAVE

STAVE SHAPING

TOPPING PLANE

HEADING VICE

INSIDE SHAVE

DOWNRIGHT

HOOP PUNCH

COOPER'S BLOCK and BLOCK HOOK

A CHIV.

AUGER

FLAG

BARREL HEAD SECTION SHOWING DOWELLED BUTT JOINTS.

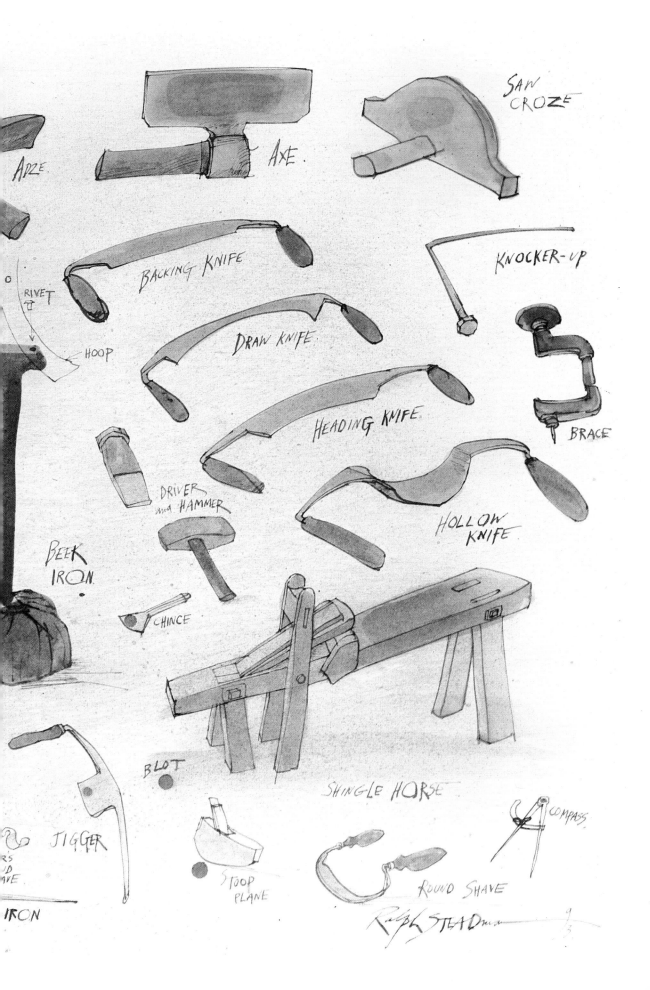

ADZE.

AXE.

SAW CROZE

BACKING KNIFE

RIVET

HOOP

DRAW KNIFE

KNOCKER-UP

HEADING KNIFE

BRACE

DRIVER and HAMMER

BEEK IRON

HOLLOW KNIFE

CHINCE

BLOT

SHINGLE HORSE

COMPASS

JIGGER

STOOP PLANE

ROUND SHAVE

IRON

Ralph STEADman

though much of the rest could be classed as central too. Scotland is full of centres of the finest, the purest, and the best of single malts, each with a distinctive claim as fervently believed in as the others, and each one central and peculiar to itself. One thing, however, these centres all have in common – the cask. In this, ethanol spirit, from every region, is matured for the minimum three years before it can claim the right to call itself whisky.

The Egyptians made straight-sided, segmented, wooden vessels, held firm with wooden hoops, 3,000 years before Christ. In Greek, Roman and Phoenician civilisations and their enclaves around the Mediterranean, terracotta clay vessels were preferred well into the first few centuries AD, though some underwater excavations have revealed barrels with hoops made from tied willow, and with the bent stave pattern. Paradoxically, coopering established itself in this part of Europe where trees are, in fact, sparse. The craft spread north, west and east where much of the best wood, from slow-growing dense forests, was to be found. The denseness, incidentally, encourages tall, straight trunks with the minimum of knots. There are over 50 species of oak tree worldwide, each species with qualities and natural tannins of its own,

THE EGYPTIAN INFLUENCE — CASK STACKING at SPEYSIDE COOPERAGE.

which interact and impart a flavour to the contents of a cooper's cask. The Romans called these casks *cupals* and their maker a *cuparius*.

The making of casks has changed little since Roman times and neither have the tools, which retain the look of ancient, but practical simplicity; only now, they are not made of stone or bronze.

Only a few oak species are favoured to fulfil all cooperage essentials – strong, tight, regular grain being the most important for ease of working. Of oak used today in Scotland 97% comes from North America (from the north-facing slopes of the Appalachian mountains, Missouri, Kentucky and Tennessee), the white oak, *Quercus Alba*, being the favourite for the light, elegant flavour it imparts to a delicate malt. Some distilleries prefer to age whisky in old casks already impregnated with oloroso sherry, for a richer, spicy, dark finish. Sessile oak from Northwest Spain is richer and more robust in flavour, as is Memel oak from Eastern Europe. Limousin oak from France is also a cooper's favourite but is used mainly for the maturation of wines. The Egyptians, incidentally, lined their barrels with tar to prevent the wood from tainting their wines, and to seal the wood.

While oak is, like all woods, porous, it resists seepage but does enable the contents to breathe.

Logs are 'quarter sawn' (see clever drawing on previous page) so that at least one dense medullary ray appears in the length and the breadth of each stave when cut to size. A medullary ray is the ring of slower winter growth that creates denser, narrow bands of cells in circles through a cross-section in the trunk. These tighter cells also resist warping. Several years of seasoning are crucial before use.

The coopers repairing old casks at the Speyside Cooperage in Craigellachie, Aberlour, in Banffshire, demonstrate to a kind of glass-enclosed spectator-balcony a labour-intensive craft, brutally hard work, minimised only by the sheer ability of the cooper and his confidence in his skills, learned over a seven-year apprenticeship. Hammering is incessant and the noise ear-shattering. Soundproofed ear-muffs are advisedly worn in the workshop itself, though some seem not to bother and are perhaps already deaf. The oldest cooper looked little more than 50 and the youngest no more than a lad. They all hammer like demons, removing old hoops called booges, quarters and chimes, and replacing them after a cask has been dismantled, damaged staves replaced, chopped with an adze, shaved with a draw knife and generally re-aligned for a perfect face-up along the edges of each stave. No extra filler should be necessary and natural, damp wood-swell will suffice to eliminate the slightest hairline crack. The conditions of sale are that the customer, the distiller, will be supplied with casks in a condition fit to fill.

A cask is not fitted together – it is 'raised up', a rather biblical phrase, I thought. At this point it looks like a wooden skirt and is ready to be fired, i.e. re-charred (see page 85).

This intensive care of a cask is reflected in its life-span of up to 60 years.

American oak barrels are often imported into the UK after having been used to mature Bourbon for up to eight years. These are 'knocked down', i.e. re-made into larger 'hogsheads' (which hold 250 litres) and sold on to store grain whisky. On a good day the cooperage can restore 400 casks to working condition again, at around £70–£90 a time. A new cask varies in price according to supply and demand but certainly costs £120 and upwards.

Shavings from refurbished casks and casks beyond repair are passed on to a salmon smoke house to end their life as fuel to smoke salmon from Scottish rivers. Some casks are put out to grass as garden tubs. Not such a pathetic end for a worthy and vital part of the Scottish whisky industry. You may sit in the dying light of evening, inside the one half, with a glass in hand looking through orange and purple splashes of everlasting pansies inside the other half, and toast the coopers whose craft lives on.

BOWMORE and BOWMORE Distillery, ISLAY.

Bowmore

The island of Islay is a mere 25 miles long by 20 miles wide. However, its 7 distilleries and 4,000 inhabitants create between them 150 million pounds of duty for the British Government, from the island's main export of single malt whisky.

The islanders are a proud but modest people, and could afford to pull up the ladder and let the rest of the world go by, if they chose. Instead, they welcome all-comers to share and enjoy their way of life, with a generosity common to people who trust in the basic goodness of others.

Bowmore, the town that gives its name to one of Islay's favourite creations, Bowmore malt whisky, is more or less a steep High Street, swooping down to the harbour from a round church at the top of the hill which has no dark corners or black holes for the Devil to hide in. Instead, the Devil hides in the distillery at the bottom of the hill, overlooking a sea which can be as rough as Scottish kneecaps, and as smooth as the whisky and the glass into which it is poured.

Bowmore is a gentle, peaty single malt, aged in oak, behind walls pounded by sea waters, driven into the bay of Loch Indaal when the Atlantic Ocean breathes itself over the land, and stretches its arms.

The cellars of Bowmore lie below sea level, and the sea's assault imparts a hint of ozone to the maturing, time-blessed nectar, lying still and mysterious in the dark. Absorbing the sea's energy, it stores it up, giving some to the angels and biding its time until the gods call out for theirs.

From a boat the building stands possessively on its own turf, where it has stood for 200 years. Its two pagoda-style peat kilns tower like fairy-tale spires, dispersing the

High St & Parish Church
BOWMORE, ISLAY: 3 Sept 91
Ralph STEADman

rich, pungent aroma of burning peat up the flared nostrils of God Himself who sighs a satisfied breeze across the land.

Not so the Devil, who lurks and smoulders in the salt-saturated darkness beneath the still house, cursing the spirit safe and its carefully controlled and protected waterfall of duty-bound treasure, pouring endlessly into the spirit receiver, and thence into heavily protected warehouse vats. From there it is dispensed into manageable casks and then sealed with a wooden bung, virtually to remain so for at least 3 years, maybe 5, maybe 10, 15, 21 and even 30 for a specially chosen batch.

The angels wait, like patient clouds on a gentle breeze, to receive their share. God, too, will be blessed with a harvest's hope, but no mention is made of the Devil. It drives him wild with rage and, as he foams, the sea pounds the cellar walls outside, casting empty barrels, like missiles assaulting this bastion, in an attempt to break through its mighty walls and devour the precious contents within.

But on occasions the Devil wins out, though not so much nowadays. Human nature became the Devil's work-horse, and many cunning ways were devised by distillery workers to extract an illicit share, something for nothing, or perhaps a little extra recompense for a job well done. If you stand for any length of time and watch the steady flow of colourless liquid pouring so freely into generous goblets, encased securely in their shining sarcophagus, the spirit safe, the mind wanders and gets to thinking that only the thickness of toughened glass stands between you and it. 'Where can it all go?' you ask yourself; 'Who shall profit?' And how could the most observant and scrupulous authority account for every last drop?

The fact is that they cannot, but they, nevertheless, try, just as those who ponder this

Bowmore Distillery – late evening 3. Sept 91.

bountiful cascade also try, to extract just enough so as not to be noticed. It adds interest to an otherwise monotonous process which is as predictable as it is precious and as easy as ABC . . .

With cunning ingenuity the Customs and Excise realised that the only way that they could prevent a distillery from cheating on this abundance was simply to make the distilleries responsible not only for the production, but also for its impeccable control. The distillers are the only ones who could possibly provide the 24-hour surveillance necessary to ensure this total security. A deal was therefore concluded with the distillers, that they would become the gaugers of their own issue and, consequently, the guardians of their own future well-being. To renege would simply be the end of the distillery. Occasional checks are made on measuring equipment and output, but the basic honesty and survival instincts of distillery managers guarantee a watertight solution, even though the Devil may still curse. The spirit is kept bonded in warehouses, duty-free, but every drop is measured and accounted for, *even the angel's share*. Perhaps that is why the Devil is never mentioned in a distillery. To name him is to invoke him. So they let him hide and they let him curse, and they blind him with light every time they unlock and open the heavy doors that keep him trapped inside . . .

Malting. Stoic Scottish islanders will plough dampened barley for at least a week, day and night, to ensure even germination before peat-smoke drying.

Malting

another 2000 gallons of Pure Malt Whisky — Ralph Steadman 91

The malting process is so old. They've been doing this for 200 years, obviously spread out on a cave floor. It's probably a fluke, like everything else. A man was probably storing his barley in a cave and it was so wet it started to shoot and he said, 'I'd better start drying this out and maybe use it.' And when he did dry it out, he found he got better whisky from it. It must have been an accident. He probably had sacks of barley and the rain was pouring down and it got wet and instead of seeing this and, being a Scotsman, being really miserable, he said, 'I don't want to waste it, I'll try to dry it. He was stubborn.'

Jim McEwan, Bowmore distillery

JURA

Sitting here in the quiet, still air with the odd noises of activity, the local bus backing up with its funny little siren, the throbbing sound of a boat, the coast guard launch, entering the harbour, the Paps going slightly dim and becoming sharp again as the mists lift and fall in the sunshine which bathes us all in its mellow, satisfied gentle sway. The fishermen have just come back in their little tug boat, for all the world like a little Pop-eye boat, and delivered lobsters in a basket onto the jetty – obviously the speciality of Port Askaig Hotel. Overlooking the little harbour, Port Askaig Stores and Post Office, established in 1767, sells petrol and oil, and general stores, and is probably a meeting place during the odd morning shop. There are very few tourists but a sufficient, steady little flow of people who have discovered such a place

as this. Sitting inside the harbour wall are two old boats – to some, an eye-sore, to others, a symbol of bravery in the last war. The old CN 82 with its barnacled, moss-dripping hull which was used to ferry men from Dunkirk and is considered to be a symbol of bravery in this region of the islands. The hotelier is not very happy having it there but the owner of the boat said that if it's good enough for carrying Dunkirk survivors back to Scotland, it's good enough to sit in a harbour as a symbol, so there it stays. And what else? The sounds of wheeling, squawking birds, hammering, knocking, people doing things all the time, not very big things, done in a certain slow, rhythmic way. The bus is off out of Port Askaig, probably back to Port Ellen, up and down the island. The island has very few roads; the main road circles it, but is

not completed. The top, northern edge doesn't have a road, maybe just a dirt track. The ferry is now back until the next trip across the Sound of Islay to Jura at three o'clock. It seems to go once every two hours and is only large enough to take six cars at the most, a truck, plus a few foot passengers. It chugs its way back and forth, the journey takes between five and ten minutes and the island of Jura is near enough for us to make it out quite clearly, the shore on the other side and the landscape.

And, of course, the excise officers were the guys who had reached the end of the road, who weren't being promoted. Imagine being consigned to Glen Whatever in 1900 – it was a fate worse than death, really. But there was a mutual trust, in a way. If an excise officer decided to make life difficult for a distillery, the distiller could make life hell for the excise man because within the Excise Act the officer couldn't interfere with production. So if the distillery manager said, 'Right, I want to take charge at four o'clock in the morning,' the excise man had to be there to oversee it, because everything had to be written down. So there was a sort of balance. What's more, the manager didn't even have to be there. He could get one of his subordinates to take charge and he could stay in bed.

Anon

There were a couple of excise officers and one of the things they had to do was take a 'regular' sample of mature whisky so that they could test their instruments. The only way they could do this was to go into the warehouse, draw some mature whisky, get up to their office – they couldn't do it anywhere else – and test their working instruments against the standard instruments. In theory, that stuff was supposed to go back into the cask, but believe me, that equipment was tested to destruction.

Anon

The KEEPERS of the QUAICH . BLAIR CASTLE

The Keepers of the Quaich

The walls of Blair Castle bear blatant testimony to a bloody thirsty and venously hungry past. The front entrance hall bristles like an army of porcupines. Guns, swords, pikes, polished bayonets and shields shroud the magnificent wood panelling. A stuffed stag sits in somnolent posture before a standing array of bayonetted rifles and a portrait of the Duke of Atholl, seated in his plus fours with a twelve-bore shotgun under his arm. Even to this day the Duke of Atholl is allowed, by legal consent, to raise a private army in times of political unrest and uncertain stability – which is really any time at all.

The Right Honourable, The Earl of Elgin and Kincardine KT, is in attendance as usual, a popular event in himself, dressed like a tartan milliner's shop, wearing the trousers in preference to the kilt. He was a previous Grand Master of the Keepers, and, so rumour has it, Chief Mason of Scotland, and he possesses more than a passing resemblance to Billy Bunter.

There were many other Billy Bunter lookalikes at this twice-a-year occasion, but most of them wore kilts. The occasion is a pretty high-flown get-together for the top men in the trade, including the distillery owners themselves. Nothing less than being piped in through the front entrance by the Atholl Highlanders will do. It is a moving experience and for about five minutes I was led to believe that I was pretty important, practically a pretender to the throne of Scotland. As I moved inside the castle, with Anna resplendent and beautiful in elegant clothes, adorned with the Keepers of the Quaich's own blue-brown tartan shawl, I felt a surge of tradition pour over me like liquid haggis.

From every wall and along every corridor towards the wedding-cake ante-chambers and the main Banqueting Hall, the skulls of antlered deer stared bleakly down at my every footstep. There must have been thousands of them, all uniform, which prompted me to speculate, between the bagpipes and the inner sanctum, how many others it would have been necessary to sacrifice to achieve such astonishing symmetry, considering nature's persistent variety.

The main Hall itself confounded my wildest speculation. The antlered skulls in there were displayed like a repeating 3D wallpaper pattern.

The Keepers of the Quaich ceremony is only traditional in its present form as a reincarnation of a clan chieftain's ceremony from earlier, more earthy days before PR companies, when a damn good fight would have been perfectly in order between courses of Haggis wi' Champit Tatties an' Bashed Neeps an' a Wee Drap o' the Cratur. They would probably have used the Roast Border Lamb as a weapon, two legs each, and would have dispensed with the Chestnut and Watercress Mousse entirely. Pudding was unheard of but it was the whisky, after all, that they would have been there for, and the settling of old scores.

To date the ceremony in its present form is only six years old and all the arm-wrestling of hard business would have been settled beforehand. The only order of the day was the induction of new Keepers, the re-affirmation of Scottish values and the enjoyment of the occasion.

Everything is intact. Ron Gonella and his ensemble take us through 'The Songs of Scotland'. The blissful pipers pipe in the Haggis, an enormous bag of crudity which, I have to confess, I love passionately. The ceremonious dinner is introduced and jollied along with songs from something called 'FEAR and TIGH', by Scotland's answer to Geraint Evans, Bill McCue, with identical whiskers on his chin and his sporran, and eyebrows to match. There is fresh salmon, dressed in white-horned origami sculpture, Lords and Ladies to the left and right, the headmaster of Eton, Dr Eric Anderson (a descendant of

Robert Burns) as our main speaker, plus Mr and Mrs Yamamoto, Patricia and John to us all, from Tokyo, the strange oriental saviours of an industry in need of some help in these troubled times. The Japanese themselves have been making whisky since 1923 but still, I believe, seek the key to the essence and mysteries of making true Scotch whisky more than, I believe, the Scots appear to need them. Nevertheless, where whisky is concerned, the Japanese, rather than attempt to copy the Scots, have decided to join them. But that is business, so I didn't ask, because it was.

Kilts, trousers, cummerbunds, bow ties, sashes, satin dresses and head-locked hairdos bobbed and bounced like elements of an animated cartoon. Just before we began there was a pause in the proceedings whilst the new Keepers were inducted into the Order of the Quaich somewhere in the castle; maybe a Scottish version of a Barmitzvah in the old torture chambers, their screams out of earshot or drowned beneath the babble of the other guests. It gave us time for our own 'illicit smoking' ritual outside in the castle grounds, along with Matthew Gloag himself, a warm and friendly man who seems to treat the whole whisky trade as a pleasant diversion from the real business of living life. I guess if the right size shoes are waiting for you before you are even born, it can engender a certain *laissez-faire* with regard to earthly matters when you arrive.

His blonde wife 'Dilly' reflected this casual warmth and seemed to do her own thing, as far as whisky was concerned anyway. I suspect that wine is a more appealing and light-hearted alternative in this distinguished family, considering that it was wine that got the Gloag family into the drinks business in the first place. Their address at Bordeaux House, Perth is surely an indication.

All the distinguished guests were finally piped into the main hall after we, the others, had shuffled and tripped to our own places, wincing smiles across tables at each other. Then, accompanied by the baritone boom of our MC explaining the wonder of it all, most other things were piped in too. Every inanimate object with some significant purpose

was piped in. Late arrivals were piped in, the lights of Old Aberdeen got a mention and even a song. More pipes for the Arbroath smokies, the Burns address to the Haggis and the terrible stabbing of the bulging icon, all to pipes. I was piped to the toilet and back again. A lady on the left of the chairman got piped for blowing her nose. Dr Eric, headmaster of Eton, was piped for his speech and we all joined in for the finale of a song of glorious 'Scotland Yet'. On the first chorus, we all stood up, for the second chorus we climbed onto our chairs, and on the third chorus we were all on the table singing like drunken barbarians. If we had done that when we first arrived we would have been arrested. We got piped off the table and the distinguished guests and Keepers were piped solemnly out of the Hall at a well-appointed time, as though standing on the table had never really happened.

All of this was an uncanny reflection, indeed, of the description by a Scotsman of Robert Burns, who said that 'when not making poetry, he was given to irreverence'.

We are urged to dress up in our finest attire, which is only ever brought out for funerals and launching ocean-going liners, and then worked up into a frenzy of tartan tunes without so much as being warned that it was really an excuse for a bagpipe karaoke. It is unnerving – but nothing brings on another thirst like unnecessary excess!

Overleaf: The Famous Grouse in full autumn plumage, symbol of one of the finer blends. I learned during my sojourn in the Highlands that the grouse lives in those parts because it can survive only on heather. Its poignant cry has been likened to a desperate comrade crying: 'Go back! Go back!'

A FAMOUS GROUSE in FULL AUTUMN PLUMAGE with apologies to my friend John HUGHES of MATHEW GLOAG

STEADman

23

BLENDING

'To say that blending whisky is just a matter of mixing together a few varieties of single malts and grain whiskies, according to a known recipe, to produce a consistent and well-known product with a standard trade name, would be to diminish the art of a blender to nothing more than a pie-maker.' The great 19th-century haggis- and pie-maker Simon Ferintosh McWall said that. Above his baking ovens he had built his own set of stills, ten in all, which worked every

time he baked bread. He had the yeast, the know-how, the contacts *and* his own network of smugglers. He made malt bread, of course, and always had surplus supplies which were steeped, germinated and then dried under cover of his legitimate business. Shipments of illicit whisky were hidden beneath tons of his venison pies and indeed their own piecrust. It always reached the Lowlands undetected. Suspicions were only roused when he was once interrupted nose-ing one of his own pies during a visit from a Weights and Measures inspector. He absent-mindedly referred to it as a fine wee dram. He

The BLENDER NOSEING

Quality CONTROL: Everything is tasted and analysed. The slightest impurity is a failure. 100% is the only standard.

became famous as the Dingwall Jail baker and then the Jailbreaker – 'a file with every pie', but I digress . . .

A blender is a man with rare powers of scent – a bloodhound of sorts who can detect the slightest foreign body and then eliminate it. His goal is to ensure that the blend of a high-quality whisky is precisely the same in each and every bottle, given that variables will inevitably occur and must be compensated for by the addition of a nuance of another distiller's spirit. The balance must be as near as a nose hair to the inherent qualities that the imbiber has come to expect from his whisky . . .

The variables are practically infinite, no matter how careful, scrupulous and exacting each individual distiller is, and they are all of that. Quality reigns supreme throughout the industry. However, nature being the heartland of all processes, changes are inevitable. Atmosphere, temperatures, humidity, water temperatures, barley, the judgement of the still manager and the workers whose task it is to know when each process is complete – all affect the final spirit. Slight changes are inevitable, but these changes are not generally defects – just differences, undetectable to the average person. However, to a blender they are a signal to adjust the blend, to compensate and, therefore, achieve the recognised consistency. The operation is about as difficult as remembering everybody's face in the crowd at Murrayfield, but a blender practically has that astonishing ability. I say practically, because several blenders work together and ask each other if something is suspect. I would place them at the very pinnacle of the art of whisky-making and nominate them the true experts in a complex world of contradiction and personal opinions.

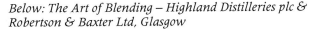

You have to tune in – at first you're not that sharp. Sometimes you can pick it up, odours come off and if you don't catch them early on you sometimes miss them. I don't drink a lot of whisky.

Whisky Blender

Below: The Art of Blending – Highland Distilleries plc & Robertson & Baxter Ltd, Glasgow

A Glen Urquhart bull broke the rule. There was a bothy above Gartalie. The cattle were always fed the draff and burnt ale which is non-alcoholic at that point. After that its alcoholic content resumes its chemical inter-action and proceeds on through its distilla-tion. The herd's bull once stumbled into the bothy which had been left unguarded after a brewing session. In washbacks the wort was fermenting furiously. The bull drank his fill. It was no longer a bull's world. The bull, full and farting, turned on the world as he saw it. So would you. A stumbling bull is not quite the same as a stumbling drunk. The first sight a bull gets of anything worth charging is the return of the very man who made the crea-ture distraught in the first place. Jarraech Bunallich had been for a wee dram other than his own in the local Breehae and he was in nae mood to tak oan anither cratur. The bull tak bee stemoch pens und grund leks itsel und thrumps afair intae the groo. Arggh! says the bothy grun. Tae, ya doon?? What? Get aff, ya muckle beastie! Too late. Po'or Jar-raech, he didnae last the nicht.

Come morning, the bull had forgotten the night before and at that very moment smelled a true cow on heat. It's how life goes on. There is no rhyme or reason to it, or fairplay, for that matter.

Highland Park

Highland Park is a kind of St Peter's Gate to its town of Kirkwall on the Orkney's, and lord of all it surveys.

Orkney's remoteness from the mainstream of whisky production enhances its sense of uniqueness. There is only one other distillery on the island – Scapa (named after the concrete-blocked Scapa Flow of World War II fame), which, I suspect, lacks nothing but investment in its ability to produce a single malt as concrete as anything that the island is famous for, including the standing stones at the Ring of Brogar, and the 5,000 year-old settlement at Skara Brae. There is a wisp of highland heather in the peatreek smoky blue flavours captured inside the pagoda-shaped bottle of Highland Park, which should just as well apply to a Scapa dram.

(The proprietor of THE SHOP in Kirkwall, purveyors of fish and foodstuffs to Her Majesty the Queen, was more than in agreement with my poetic assessment as I purchased his own brand of peaty haggis which exploded in the baggage hold on our return flight via Aberdeen. I found a suitable replacement at Martin's of George Street in Aberdeen, a tip for those who go haggis-hunting when in the neighbourhood.)

HIGHLAND PARK Distillery → approaching KIRKWALL, ORKNEY

SCAPA

In fact, a bottle of Scapa turned up at Heathrow airport, where we were on our way to Lyon to make a pilgrimage to Burgundy country. Scapa 10 year-old single malt is a fine dram, a flawless echoed dream of lapping waves against the peated, rocky beaches of the Lingro Burn from whence it came, resonating in some foreign clime like a reassuring friend, and no more so than in the damp country air of Brouillard just outside Beaune. Here, in the Hostellerie du Vieux Moulin, which my editor, who was in the same jam as me, renamed the Hostility of Mutton dressed as Lamb, the honest, salty strength of the Scapa kept us honour-bound to hold our blunder on course and suffer yet another three nights in that Nouvelle Amex bunker, which managed to lose another Michelin star as we tried to figure out whether the chef wanted to satisfy our raging hunger or teach us quantum physics with wafer-thin sliced carrots and radiating spirals of mangetout peas. Scapa replaced the Knockando (my choice from some promotion-pushy honker in the duty-free shop), but later made a rather interesting blend. Adding the bourbon sweetness of the Knockando forged a strange and evocative marriage which lent another dimension to the Scapa, but would probably make an Orcadian emigrate to Greenland and weep blocks of ice. Nevertheless it broke our shackles, strengthened our resolve – and with one mighty leap we were free!

The Queen was here in 1980 – that's the Queen's barrel there. It's been maturing since then and we've informed the keeper of the royal cellar. I would think they'll take the barrel. It will be interesting to find out if they are going to charge the Queen any duty on it.

Jim McEwan, Bowmore distillery

STRATHISLA Distillery, Keith, Banffshire.

ARDBEG Distillery Islay

Lagavulin Distillery, ISLAY (home of WHITE HORSE) (and a SMUGGLER'S HAUNT) Ralph Steadman 91

LAPHROAIG →

Of the survivors from the 1745 Jacobite Rebellion, three brothers – the Johnstons of the Clan MacIan (MacDonald), from Ardna-murchan, left the mainland and arrived in Islay to find work. They all became farmers and distilled their own whisky – a practice more common on Islay than anywhere else in Scotland. The sons of one brother settled at Laphroaig and started a small distillery about 1812. One was diligent and went legal in 1826 and had bought the other out by 1836, remaining a tenant on land owned by the Campbells.

He died by what could be described as a brewer's death of the thousand gulps. He fell into a vat of burnt ale and lived only two days after, but he did set the record for the longest pee in history. He left a second wife and six children, two of them sons who were far too young to run a distillery. The business was leased to another distillery, Lagavulin, just a couple of hundred yards down the road, until Dugald, the youngest son, became old

enough to take over, which he did in 1857, with the guidance of Lagavulin. They remained his agents until 1907, though Dugald himself had already gone to the great distiller in the sky in 1877. He left no heirs.

Now, I appreciate that this is a bit of a saga so you'll have to concentrate. *His* sister Isabella, right?, had married *his* brother Alexander Johnston of Tallant (whoops! though I might be mistaken) who ran the distillery for his wife, and *her* other three sisters who had a share in the business. OK? Now, Isabella died and husband Alexander inherited *her* share, but *he* died too in 1907, leaving a hell of a legal mess behind. This was the stuff of TV soap dramas. Court case followed court case. *Two* of the three sisters were finally awarded ownership but one of them had married a William Hunter. *He* had a nephew, a Glasgow tram engineer called J. Johnston Hunter, who *also* now got a piece of the action.

However, it was Mrs William Hunter's son, Ian, who after finishing his training as an engineer on the mainland, hastily returned to Islay in 1908 and controlled the business on behalf of his mother and *her* sister, *his*

Aunt Katherine. The distillery appears to have flourished between 1877 and the turn of the century and much building was done during that time. Then, at the time of Alex Johnston's death in 1907, things seem to have got in a bit of a pickle (and if this had been a TV drama there would have been a murder just about here). Son Ian reckoned that the Mackie family who owned Lagavulin had not been too generous as agents and he broke off business relations with them. After a blazing row Mr Mackie went beserk and got his men to pull out the foundation stones of Laphroaig's water source, effectively cutting it off.

I know from personal experience (and Thomas Hardy!) that some country people do dumb spiteful things like that. I have had access to my own cesspit obstructed for nearly five years now. I do not want to distil its contents of course, but if it is left much longer, we could have a mini Mount Etna lava flow on our hands which could threaten a third of Kent. But I digress . . .

Following another court case, Mr Mackie of Lagavulin had to repair the damage and restore the vital water supply, but not before enticing Laphroaig's master brewer away to make malt whisky for him. (Yet another twist for my TV drama.) The strange thing is, and it *is* the case in many other such situations of close proximity, that even using the same type of pot still *and* the same water, *and* even the same brewer, Mr Mackie could not make the same 'peatreek' whisky – a mere 200 yards away on the same coast. And whilst I am on the subject, neither is Ardbeg whisky the same just 200 yards further on from Laphroaig, in the other direcion. It is still an intriguing mystery today and confounds absolute scientific analysis, though experts harumph amongst themselves that it is merely a matter of natural variants, and so it is, but a mystery of nature nevertheless. In fact, so patently obsessed with maintaining continuity and consistent quality are all individual distillers, that, when they install a new still, they will even have the same dents and peculiarities bashed back into it just in case it is those blemishes which influence a distinctive taste. Now, try and tell me *that* is a scientific procedure, but I digress yet again.

Meanwhile (back in our new TV drama),

Laphroaig Distillery (The beautiful hollow by the broad bay).

the court cases nearly broke Laphroaig, but Ian Hunter was a good businessman and bought the land from new owners in 1921, the Ramsays of Kildalton, and from under the very nose of Mr Mackie himself, who even then tried to outbid Ian Hunter. Finally, each of the three distilleries bought their own land and their squabbles settled down to a pleasant bitchy co-existence. Laphroaig increased its production capacity with the help of their new agents, Robertson and Baxter, to double its previous output.

In 1927 Ian Hunter went completely independent and started to sell direct, probably after the death of his other partners, his cousin the tram engineer, in 1922, and his Aunt Katherine in 1927, leaving him and his mother as sole owners. The Johnston Hunters seem to have been quietly giving up the ghost or perhaps taking to the spirit. Families are funny things and only ever really show up when there is a will to be read or a wedding to attend, and, of course, Christmas.

His mother died in 1928 and Ian Hunter ran it entirely alone until 1950 when he became a limited company and made himself Managing Director until his death in 1954 (and that's good for a couple of episodes, and so is the next bit). His secretary, Miss Williamson, became Managing Director and ran the place with the efficiency of a humming bird until it fell into the hands of Long John in 1967. But *she* must have been quite some character, a backroom matriarch perhaps, who guided Ian Hunter's decisions like a Scottish Joan Collins. (In fact in *my* TV drama Miss Williamson takes over Long John, Matthew Gloag *and* United Distillers and sets up her power base on Islay, the Dallas of the Western Isles, eventually becoming Life Grand Mistress of the Keepers of the Quaich and Lady Malt of Jura, because she stayed single all her life. It's a winner and by the time you read this, we will be half way through the production schedule of

September Heather

BIG L – The Saga of Distilled Illicit Passions in the Whisky Business.) In real life, however, Miss Williamson remained Laphroaig's Chairman and Managing Director until she retired in 1972. An intriguing life history of just one distillery, more because of what is left out than what is put in. (There are over 180 others. I could keep the series going for years!)

I once threw a party for the launch of my illustrated version of *Treasure Island* at my local pub in Loose, Kent because I had used the pub as the model for The Admiral Benbow in the book. I remember the slogan for the party. It was 'GET LEGLESS ON LONG JOHN'. I wonder if they remember, because we don't.

LAIRD: Now gentlemen – am I to understand that we intend to drink like gentlemen?
GUEST: Of course, sire, of course!
LAIRD: Good man; then we can get as drunk as farts!

Duty was imposed on spirits unfairly in relation to beer because the brewers were the biggest supporters of the Tory Government. They gave masses of funds to the Government 150 years ago. They were keeping the brewers happy.

Anon

There was an old spirit safe in one distillery which once had a tube welded into it which led to a nearby pub, so that they could take the whisky straight from the spirit safe into the pub and serve it to customers. There is a lot of evidence that this actually happened.

Anthony Troon, Journalist

The River Laggan, Islay.

The contribution per individual worker is enormous, in terms of what they generate for the Exchequer in potential duty, not to mention the value of exports – about £1.8 billion.

John Hughes, Highland Distillers

The coopers were better to keep clear of the drams because they didnae last ony time . . . The manager, the first thing he asked me was if I was teetotal. Like I say, as far as whisky's concerned, it disnae worry me – I take it if I need it.

The late Davy Bell, Retired Cooper, Bowmore distillery

It's like the salmon in the rivers, the Scots have never believed they belong to the landowners. For the same reason they've never believed that the whisky belongs to the distillers.

Anthony Troon, Journalist

Davy Bell. Passed away on December 17th, 1993, at the age of 96. One of whisky's great characters, a cooper for 52 years, he is at present helping the Great Distiller in the Sky to get it how he likes it.

4 Smugglers and Guagers of Terse and Ruthless PEDIGREE

Men and women of gritty and brutal intensity ran amok at the turn of the 19th century. Overnight it went from Scottleland to Bottleland and the heather heaved with the feverish activity of steaming hideyholes, wherever a pot still could be secreted and hidden within minutes to avoid discovery.

SHORTAS LARGYBEG DROON, though slow-witted, used his slow ways to invent a system of distillation that was continuous, saved time and which he kept going for 45 years though he never saved any of the whisky. That was perhaps the nature of his slowness. The whole process was arranged along the bank of a fast-flowing burn above Loch Snizart along the western coast of Skye. Water would go in through a catch funnel at one end and mix with his own mucky brown wort. He would then boil it, ferment it, percolate it like coffee through his tube labyrinth, moofle it off as alcoholic steam into an antechamber, and cool it through a submerged zigzag worm before belching it out into the burn again further down the glen. Those folk using the burn below his still walked in a perpetual stupor and never knew a sober day from birth to death. Shortas Droon pre-dated Robert Stein and Aeneas Coffey with their 'patent' continuous still inventions by at least 26 years, though Droon was never credited with anything but slowness.

WEE TOMMY WETKNEDDLIE did absolutely nothing for the smuggling trade but claimed blood ties with everyone. An inveterate liar, he told touring parties anything they wanted to believe in exchange for a wee dram. He had his uses, though, since he would often blab all manner of lies to roaming excise men who would take him at his word and stagger off in another direction on the strength of a new clue. He wore a patch only to elicit more sympathy and for dramatic effect, though it was, in fact, his purse in which he kept the King's shilling, though never found a need to spend it. He claimed he gave his sporran to Bonnie Prince Charlie to express his generosity and loyalty.

JOCKLER BARLEYCORN McVAIG grew the finest barley and from it produced the silkiest peatreek though he was a farmer first who loved the land and a still man second because he loved the drink. He could only grow the best barley when he was drunk and only got poetry out of a still when he was gravestone sober. His wife Ellie would only have him in the house when he was between those two states – 'when the man can gae me a sensible leer', she said. The gaugers never caught him. He was far too drunk to talk to when he tilled his land and when he was at his still he was far too sober to let a gauger catch him at it. He was known as a well-rounded fellow.

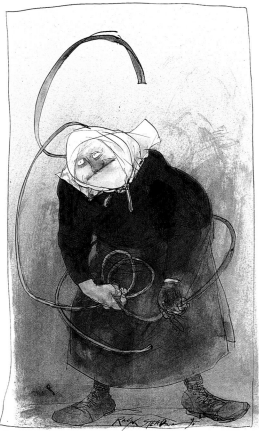

*GAY GORDON FANBUGGERY was
never told whether she was a man or a
woman. The product of relentless
inbreeding, Gay was weaned as a boy
since the Fanbuggerys had already got
twelve daughters. Gay grew as tough
as a man in a skirt and learned to arm
wrestle and drink with the smugglers
who frequented the Tilted Wig on the
Isle of Muck. The only time she used
her feminine charms was when there
came a visit from the gaugers which
has to be said was rare. As they came
ashore Gay would stand full square on
the end of the jetty, flex her muscles
enticingly and spit on the capstan until
they turned around and went away.
She was much praised by all
smugglers for what they referred to as
her art of seduction. In this way she
fulfilled her womanhood without
losing her heart to any man.*

*PIPEWORM LOLA CLATTIE was
courted by many a still man for her
amazing pipework. She could
magically wind a worm through any
burn, transforming it into what
appeared to be virtual undergrowth to
a passer-by. Many an angler has
cursed her very name on getting his
tackle tangled with Lola's mangled
wangle pipe network – a miracle of
plumbing ingenuity in perpetuity . . .
She was patronised by royalty who
commissioned her to design the
pipework for the organ in the private
chapel at Balmoral.*

*PEABROCH GWENNIE BAGDHU
distilled her wort through bagpipes
and played pure Pibroch pipe music as
the vapours condensed. She believed
that the very soul of Scotland entered
the spirit as it passed through her
beloved instrument. She had her own
technique of playing, developed over
the years through her suck-blow
counterpoint harmonic drone and
scalic progressions which vibrated
through the vapours creating a
cacophony of pure liquid music.*

Nobody else can produce Highland Park whisky. You could set
up a distillery in, say, Tunbridge Wells, get the same kind of
barley, import the water from Orkney, make the mash, ferment it, distil it in the same-shaped stills, put it in the same
barrels, let it mature for the same length of time, and it would
still taste like kangaroo piss. You will never be able to explain
that chemically.

Anthony Troon, Journalist

SHERLOCK MACBHU was a master of disguise and many swore he could blend with the landscape into virtual invisibility. But none missed his eyes or his socks, only when it was too late and he was upon them. His eyes were bloodshot orange and his socks were adorned with the fur of white rabbits. Macbhu rarely slept – he could not, knowing that even one bothy bubbled and glooped profit into the smuggler's palm. Finally he did go to sleep on the banks of Loch Ness after his ten thousandth arrest, and 'tis said that his ghost is about when the mists rise and the banks of the Loch are chequered in tartan.

BLACK ANGUS GLENBLACKLAS took no quarter from anyone nor did he give any. His heart was blacker than his name. His glowering black eyebrows were enough to strike the very curse of black granite into the soul of any man. He was as bald as he was black and he hid his only guilty secret beneath a glowing lock of black eyebrow swept over his pate and tied with a black bow. He carried a blackguard's stick with the head of a bald vulture on its top which he brandished like a claymore. The vulture's beak could transform a useful copper still into a worthless colander in a matter of minutes with a thousand 'holes of enlightenment' as he used to refer to them. He is still alive and lives in Blackheath.

MUCKLEY MCSHONACH, one of the many excise officers who ultimately fell victim to the enticements and rare temptations of some of the finest illicit malts that were ever made. Some were undrinkable and their makers would feel the full force of Muckley's Law, while some of the truly classic malts became their bargaining chips of survival for those who were artists of their craft. Men like Muckley McShonach could never resist a tempting wee dram – 'though only a wee one, mind.' There was much work to be done. The bothy boys were forever busy. Muckley finally expired like an oil tanker in a massive fireball of inflammable vapours when he fell backwards into a hidden bothy before the very eyes of the smugglers themselves who never drank another drop to his memory.

There's no duty on a shotgun!
Anon

The
EXCISE
MAN.

SMUGGLING

It was the wretched English who started it.

It was they who wantonly provoked the widespread distillation of whiskies of great individual distinction in the Highlands. It was they, the bloodsucking, violent, kleptomaniac English who imposed unreasonable taxes on a home-made nectar, the lifeblood of a proud, god-fearing breed, hell-bent on minding their own business.

It was the English, the cunning, avaricious Empire-building English, who imposed the tax on the very raw material that made whisky possible, the barley malt. If they had not been so blinded by jealousy, the power-hungry Hanoverian government of 1713 would have taxed the babbling waters, too, that lend Scotland's national drink its character and a velvet charm that is smoother than the rump of a young gelding in fettle.

It was the English who spitefully stabbed at

the very heart of a timeless Gaelic tradition, in a fit of twisted pique, as the demand for whisky grew and wine and brandy lapsed in popularity.

In defiance, the private still proliferated in every barn and every hole in the ground that Highlanders could find. To these people, the farmers and crofters, it was against reason to put a tax on the fruits of the earth and sea which were, after all, god-given, to be enjoyed by all, rich and poor. They should not be subjected to the laws of man. It was an heroic age. To outwit the excise man, the gaugers and the English army, who supported them, became a matter of honour. 'Freedom and Whisky gang thegither,' wrote Robert Burns, a poetic excise officer, giving the Scots a battle-cry steeped in the springs of moral indignation and the knowledge of a clear difference between simple law-breaking and a genuine sense of wrong. The inaccessibility of the hidden stills of Glenlivet and the secret hill-pony trails to the Lowlands led to heady intrigue and forged brave hairy men of traditional pedigree, and a drink with as many styles as there were stills.

The Excise Man. Many unkind things have been written about this official and I have no business trying to portray him unless I have something new to add. Much of the criticism has been unfair but much of it is justified. And it's more than my job's worth to leave him out. He will remain an irresistible figure of fun who could, nevertheless, strike terror into the hearts of those who would persist in breaking the law.

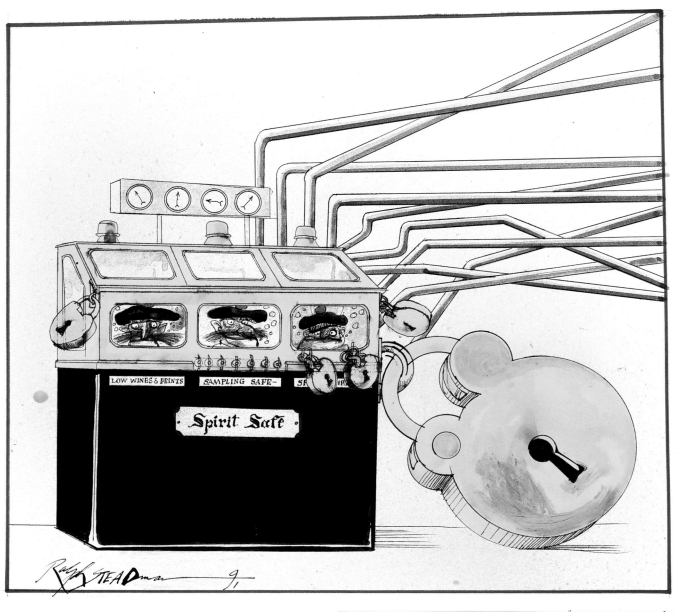

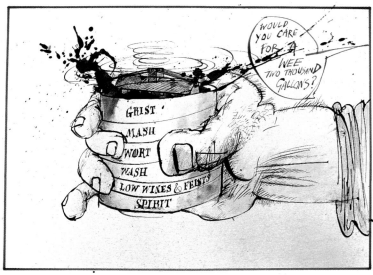

Another excise officer at a certain distillery, which was the first one to tanker whisky direct from the distillery to where they wanted to blend it. There was Tanker No. 1, and Tanker No. 2 and the excise officer was known as Tanker No. 3.

Anon

It would be three days before I came within a mile of friendly life and I had to avoid the gaugers at all costs. Faithful Fiddich, my hill pony, stumbled a moment and then steadied her sturdy wee frame under the weight of 28 gallons of prime Podwillie's peatreek. The rocky path took a steep turn downwards and I was forced to restrain Fiddich's pace and hold onto the wobbling bags. It was getting dark, and the heather was glowing purple, as the green turned black against the orange sunset.

'What's up, Fidd? You seem a wee bit strange.' A disturbed grouse fluttered and cried out, 'Go back! Go back!' flying off towards the dying light. The beast stopped dead in her tracks and glanced round at me, as if to scold me for being the cause of her discomfort. The look in her eye told me volumes, and she began to shake. 'Gaugers! Where are they, my beauty?' I looked about nervously, as Fiddich's tail swung into action and flailed in all directions, first upwards, then to the left and, then, to the right, backwards the way we had come and into the upright position again, stiff as a flagpole at morning parade. 'You mean we're surrounded?'

As I spoke, the heather, as far as the eye could see, rose up like a spectre, a prickly mass of once-blissful landscape, on the move, no longer my beloved highlands, but a whole battalion of loathsome, living, breathing retribution, officialdom and restraint, advancing towards me like a nightmare of drowning in bad whisky itself . . .

The next moments were a blur as my fear took hold of me and Fiddich staggered as she felt it. With an instinct born of an habitual life of deceit and secrecy, Fiddich carried me and 28 gallons of incriminating evidence, like a rampant Pegasus, straight towards the advancing heather. The heather stopped in its tracks as this formidable, trundling cargo of panic charged, blindly, on a downhill path. Startled minds, with but one single thought,

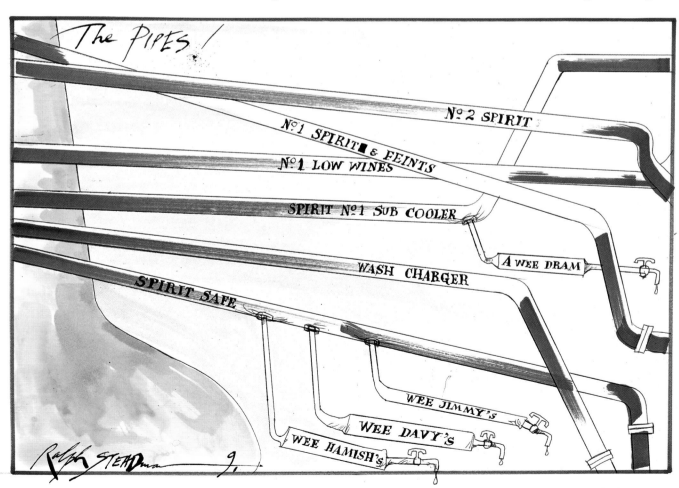

Whisky TRAIL

'TIS TRUE, THAT A WEE DONKEY COULD CARRY AT LEAST 20 gallons of ILLICIT MOUNTAIN DEW TOGETHER WITH THE WEE FREELANCER OF THE GLENS *HIMSELF* OVER HARD AND TERRIBLE TERRAIN. DOWN THEY WOULD COME FROM A REMOTE WHISKY BOTHY NEAR A HIGHLAND SPRING 'AWAY FROM PRYING EYES', AYE! AND 'TIS TRUE, SO I'M TOLD, THAT THE SAME WEE DONKEY COULD ALSO SMELL THE NERVOUS ODOUR OF THE EXCISEMAN AT ONE HUNDRED YARDS — AND RAISE ITS TAIL TALL AND STRAIGHT AS A SCOTTISH FLAGPOLE — A TIMELY WARNING THAT DANGER WAS NEAR. —

reacted. It was as though the landscape was split asunder and moved apart like the waters of the Red Sea. The unexpected movement had taken the party by surprise and, before it could rid itself of its wretched diguise, Fiddich and I were well away – us, and the grouse, melting into the valley of a tree-shrouded burn, safe as we will ever be or, at least, until dawn.

Smugglers were the true pioneers of the whisky trade. It was the constantly varied locations, the hurried processes, the fear, the persistence of the smugglers to pursue their craft and hone their skills, and their utter preoccupation with the nature of whisky that instilled into the Scotsman's character the desire to be the best distillers in the world. Using pure unadulterated malt, smugglers did much to improve the quality and style of the whiskies they created.

When the history of the 20th century is written, the drug smugglers will not be so favourably acknowledged, but it will not be entirely their fault. The resistance by society to other stimulants has created a hideous blind spot, an inability to see any connection whatsoever between the effects of alcohol and their social context and the effects of drugs and their social context. The one was legalised and the other is ostracised. Therefore there can be no control on drugs, and even less on the streets. One man's crack becomes another man's poison. But I digress . . .

The smugglers did the groundwork for today's whisky distillers. Without the 1823 Act, there probably wouldn't be an industry as we know it today.

To put down the illicit activity, harsh legislation was enacted, whereby whole townlands on which any portion of a still, wash, low wines or other materials for distillation were found were punished collectively. The fines imposed were spiteful and crippling and yet those punished complained that all they knew in life was distillation and thereby claimed it to be their only means of subsistence, and even their birthright.

Bothies were therefore constructed on the borders of towns in mountain caves on island lakes, or on boats in rivers. Revenue officers were kidnapped and hidden for weeks on end to prevent them giving testimony – and whilst the liquor was processed and disposed of profitably. The captive revenue men were also forced to work on the batches of distilled liquor as an added indignity.

Today, it is extremely difficult to walk anywhere in the Highlands without stumbling into an overgrown hole which was once a bothy. We should re-open them and develop tourist bothies. Curious passers-by could enter into a kind of nether world where they would re-enact the smugglers' role and get caught in the act, thus adding an unexpected twist to their adventure holiday.

In Ireland it was rather different. There great mounds of potatoes hid crouched men and peaty fires in trenches and damp ditches as they set about their work. The potatoes would be crushed raw and boiled low and long in huge iron pots to make a mash. After yeasting the distilling proper began and fiddlers evoked the spirits with a jig or two, increasing the tempo as the wort in the still reached boiling point. It put music into the very potheen itself. 'Dat war a bum note you was playing thur, O'Shaughnessy' . . . 'Don't tell me I war playin' a bum note! Tak that yo swoyn!!' and often a fight broke out right in the middle of the best cut. The still would topple over in the struggle and all would be lost save the foreshot, the low wines, which was weaker than the rest. O'Shaughnessy's Bum Note was the name given to any inferior potheen that was offered for sale from under a peatreeking old coat.

THE SCREECH OWL Deep in the lonely hours of a bothy night, the cry of the Screech Owl leeched fear from the moon and cooled the bones of a terrified bothy man. Sometimes it was only the scream of vapours escaping through a pinprick leak in a homemade still. Only the fear of discovery was real.

LAUGHING JACK MCSHAGBASKETT, the Che Guevara of bucket-shop peatreek peddling, knew no boundaries or moral wrong and used his still as a revolutionary weapon. He wielded its creation like liquid gunpowder, the undisputed nitroglycerine of its age. It was so volatile it exploded on impact with a gauger's pick axe, distributing his parts like raptors' offal across the heather, or a salmon's titbit in a babbling burn on its way south from whence the poor wretch had come.

The customs accept the loss of 2% plus 3% for evaporation. If it was about 10 years old, it would be 20%, plus 3%. If a barrel bursts, we have to write to the Customs & Excise and ask if they'll come and examine the cask and give the reason for the loss and we then ask them to waive the duty on that cask.

Jim McEwan, Bowmore distillery

19th Century WHISKY STILL ("A Bothy").

PEATREEK ANNIE LANDRODDUCH loved smoking, and she was 95 years old before the gaugers found out why and what she smoked. Peatreek Annie smoked peat and sat stolidly out-of-doors in all weathers over a secret bothy disguising the peat rising from her voluminous skirts. She smoked for three years before even attempting to distil whisky, to ensure that the gaugers knew exactly that the smoke came from her pipe and not from the illegal activity. She forbade her husband to distil, also to establish the illusion, which fooled the Government's officers for nearly 50 years. In all that time she only caught fire twice. There was a popular saying at the time to describe a notorious gauger, that 'his soul was as black as Peatreek Annie's knickers!'. People knew instinctively that that would be a gauger to avoid.

Malevolent hatred fueled the activities of barefooted BERYL MACHRIHANISH, no Springbank Chicken, but a sworn enemy of the English Revenue Officers who gave her a wide berth. She would spit in the eye of anyone who came within ten yards of her smouldering frame. Her apparent inability to move on account of the cold gave her a foil of insidious deceit. She served as a decoy for those who carried the actual contraband, and was perfectly happy, or indescribably miserable as suited her nature, to sit and entice the curiosity of suspicious gaugers.

AULD JEAN O'BLADDER HA!, one of the most formidable of the peatreek smugglers, was no mean adversary for the ever attentive gaugers. Secreted about her person were gallons of illicit whisky in bladders slodging about like catheters of urine. If necessary, she would use them as weapons and blind those who interfered with her underclothing as they went about their duties searching for the forbidden spirits. She was famous in Dundee.

Robert Burns, an ex-customs man, ladies' man and imbiber, extols the virtues of Highland malt:

But bring a Scotsman frae his hill,
Clap in his cheek a Highland gill,
Say, such is Royal George's will,
An' there's the foe,
He has nae thought but how to kill
Twa at a blow!

Tam o' Shanter cries out:
Wi' tippenny we fear nae evil;
Wi' Usquebae we'll face the devil.

YOUNG KEN INVERDUNK, a cooper who served the smuggling trade well. He invented the first false-bottomed barrel to hide the illicit product of his farmer friends around Elgin when John Smith went legal. He conceived the idea that if every legal barrel he made looked a certain size it would not be noticed that he had built in another 20% for peatreek – call it 'the angels' share' he would say to justify his dishonesty.

LEMMUCH KNOCKLADDIE was a guide for recruits to the smuggling trade. Dimly uncommunicative, he would send the gaugers off in the wrong direction along a well-worn path, by silently pointing his knobble stick, then beckon glumly to his young compatriots to follow him in safety. His expression never changed and many referred to him as 'the man wi' the Pot Still Face'.

BLIND BAG CRIEFF MOGRAN, known for the size of his sporran which was used to secrete illicit peatreek whisky. He would stumble about for days under its weight and his shortsightedness. As long as the path went downwards, he reckoned, he must eventually reach the lowlands and the receivers' secret depot. To return home he merely stumbled back uphill or hitched a ride on a donkey that knew the way.

In the old days, the tricks they used to get up to. The hot water bottle was a favourite round the waist, and salad cream bottles with a bit of string around them; drop the bottle in the cask, pull it with the wee bit of string, have a wee dram, and then put the top back on. Or the rubber tube round the waist, filled with whisky. Ingenious methods. For cheek a man called Big Angus was the best. They opened a cask and were grogging away. Everybody else had a wee something but Angus hadn't got a bottle, though he had a pair of wellingtons on. They got the salad cream bottle and used it to fill up the wellies. Now Angus had a very bad hip and always dragged a leg anyway and when the Customs man, standing at the gate said to him, "How's it going, Angus?" Angus limped past, saying, "Och, the hip's giving me the very devil of a pain today."

Jim McEwan, Bowmore distillery

THE EDRADOUR

3rd February, 1994

A tasting of this distinctive little malt, on the shores of Paphos on the island of Cyprus. It was 5.30 pm local time when we claimed room 352 at the Imperial Beach Hotel. We had travelled most of the day. I looked out across the sea. The sun emerged on the horizon like a fierce red boil, erupting through the purple black flesh of a threatening storm-heavy sky, spread out across a wet blanket of Mediterranean gloom.

'Told you I'd show you a good time', gasped Anna spontaneously. Anna has a way with words and was busy getting her diary started. I needed three things right away – the toilet, ointment for my first ever haemorrhoid, a shower, a walk around our immediate surroundings, a swim in the low-lit indoor pool, a long hot bath to appease my second need and a stiff drink. That's seven needs and that's life, but not a bad opening for a whisky tasting.

At a time like this only The Edradour will do. Edradour is the smallest distillery in Scotland, claiming that the minimum-sized stills, their own (500 gallons per charge) produce the best, most intense and concentrated drop of poetry in the southern Highlands just above Perth. This is not quite true. The best drop of sheer poetry, according to tradition and poetic license, was always produced in a squarer-shaped still of only 41 gallons, 2 pints, and 13 16ths, approximately, secreted in heather-bound hideaways miles from any-

where, but who is to know? It's all a pack of personal folk tales and supposition and many a duty-free dram was coaxed from the crudest utensil that never saw the light of legend beyond the luckiest few. Rumour has it that the secretion from the lymph node of a stag in rut, added to an illicit charge in the heat of the moment, transforms an otherwise normal high-quality dram into nothing less than the sweat of excitement refreshed in the baths of Aphrodite. But don't quote me on that. The Scots have an uncanny knack of reducing even a love goddess's Olympian consummations to nothing more than an excuse for scandalous behaviour. Aphrodite was, after all, a blacksmith's wife and in Scotland you can still get married over a blacksmith's anvil in Gretna Green, but not to Aphrodite, merely to the love of your life, some mortal Amazon from your own dream factory. The drink, however, The Edradour, in spite of Scottish pride and an over-indulgent use of Scottish reserve, remains Godlike – a nectar for the aforementioned moment to which I have just alluded – in room 352.

LEDRUM SNITTY, an islander who never lost his ability to snitch on his best mates. He seemed to be able to gain their trust, have them tell all and then shop them. He was from St Kilda in the Outer Hebrides and came to seek his fortune on the mainland. His shifty ways suited him well as a look-out man for the sma' still men. He was granted safe passage by the British for his inside help during the Clearances, when whole communities were forcibly ejected from their crofts to seek whatever fate had in store for them. His knowledge of their ways proved invaluable to the officers in charge of this terrible persecution, and cunning and deceit became his stock in trade. He journeyed east until at last he came to Balblair where illicit distilling activity was intense. His shiftiness appealed to the bothy men who thought it was on account of his being on the run, as indeed they were. Within the  *space of two years he had shopped every illicit distiller around the Cromarty Firth and then south as far as Fort William at the southern tip of Loch Ness. You might say he was the original Loch Ness Monster – far too shifty to be real. It was when he started snitching on the gaugers that the double subterfuge made things too hot for him. He was attempting to make his way back home across the Isle of Skye when he encountered a still in full production on the shores of Loch Harport. He could find no one to tell and began gibbering to himself out loud. He was overheard and set adrift in a small dinghy with enough provisions to get him to the Hebrides. Whether he ever made it no one knows and it turned out that no one cared. If he ever did make it home everyone had been cleared out anyway and he could never snitch on anyone again.*

The story was that they used to walk with the coffin. The coffin had handles on the side, as they do. They'd stop for a rest and put the coffin down and two men would take their place. The two men in the middle went to the front and two new ones would come in at the back. So they were constantly changing. When they stopped they would have a fairly large dram with the cortège behind. On one occasion they got to the graveside and found they'd left the coffin behind on the road somewhere!

Jim McEwan, Bowmore distillery

Amos Andromach, 12th Earl of Buckie, Baron of Strathbogie, 3rd chief of the Clan Knockdromach, 7th Hereditary Lord High Constable of Scotland, Senior Great Officer and Royal Household Interpreter of all Legal Situations as he saw them, Judge Logie Coldburn of that Ilk, and Jury of Migvie, Lord Lyon King of Claymores – and Smuggler. His family motto was 'Nae a Drap went by that didna catch ma' Eye'. The most brutal of Speyside gentry, he administered the law like a lava flow to scour out every wee hint of 'Bothic misdemeanour'. Most arrested Bothy men were shipped to the Colonies and he eliminated as he went about his sacred duties every likely source of competition to his own illicit indiscretions. Respected beyond reason through fear and bribery, he created an empire of bubbling riches and was an advocate of the Hanoverian Malt Tax as a perfect front for his own activities. He was also a lay preacher and installed a pot still beneath the pulpit in the church and in the mausoleums of families on his blackmail list. He died peacefully in his bed, aged 110 years of age, inhaling the vapours of sin beneath it. It was claimed that the peaty fumes were good for his asthma and the purification of his dark soul.

Aberdeen Angus Dromtochie was the kindest of highland bothy minders and the worst distiller north of Strathspey on account of his insistence on the use of bulldung as a barley smoke drier and a straight worm to condense the pungent reek of his wort. But these were desperate times in the early 19th century and the gaugers were moving in with their growing knowledge of a smuggler's tricks. Burning bulldung did not arouse suspicion like peat and Angus flooded the market with his foul potion which some say tasted like burned caramel, but many likened it to bulldung, lacking the poetic imagination of Angus himself who called it Angel's Water. His reputation for kindness stemmed from his habit of giving his issue away at every available opportunity. It was the last drink offered to condemned men before they went to the gallows, being, as it was, free and therefore a smart economic move by officers of the British government who shamelessly pocketed the revenue otherwise earmarked for such grisly expenditure. Angus died poor but happy that he had sent some poor wretch on his last journey heaving a sigh of relief.

Wobbling Henry Mullfarclas (known as Hernia Mullfarclas) developed a strange walk from years of carrying gallons of peatreek down to the lowlands for dispersal over the borders. His donkey died and he never replaced it but instead attempted to carry as much as the donkey could when it was alive as a mark of respect. Henry loved animals on account of their stupidity which Henry considered to be a useful attribute and prided himself on being more stupid than the donkey himself. On this point Henry was very wise.

ONE-EYED KILTIE DAN CODDMUGGLER survived Culloden with the loss of only one eye and swore the English would pay through the nose forever. Smuggling became his profession as the most likely activity to cheat the English. His language was foul and his peatreek left drinkers speechless, scouring their mouths out like farmyard buckets. Many was the time he would entice the gaugers to catch him to find out which of them had 'the weakness', that tendency to turn a blind eye in exchange for a wee piece of the natural product. His one eye would fix them with a laser look and he would feign to bring out his most secret stock of his finest drop and urge a victim to knock it back whilst they had the chance. On doing so a luckless gauger would sink into a state of shock, roll his eyeballs through 180 degrees and blunder backwards blind with pain and panic. Most never returned since the brain would no longer recall where on earth it was they first encountered One-eyed Kiltie and neither did they want to . . .

TWO-EYED KILTIE COM CODMUGGLER was One-eyed Kiltie's son who idolised his father because of his war exploits and his ruthless ways. Two-eyed Kiltie emulated his father and produced an even more scouring brew which was yet more violent since he built in a delayed action honey syrup which took effect half an hour later when it attacked the bladder and the lower intestine like a ballistic laxative. Trousers were often blown apart in the violent eruptions and hypothermia of the lower parts was inevitable in the midst of winter. As the gauger ran for his life and hope of shelter, Two-eyed Kiltie would shout his father's old battlecry after him in contempt, 'Och aye! There goes the Kiltless Battle Charge!!'

There was a big difference between what was considered simple, straightforward law breaking and a moral wrong, which most considered a real crime. The English took the drink from the Scots by imposing a tax that the poor could not pay – hence the strong illicit distilling which was carried out with strong moral indignation.

Alexander, Duke of Gordon, persuaded the Government to see reason – to reduce the unreasonable duties and thereby persuade the Highlanders, those whose drink had been a natural part of life, that all could be done above board and within reason.

And so in 1823, an act sanctioning the making of whisky 'at a reasonable duty' was introduced. Small private stills were made illegal, but some were such good ones and so well-sited for the water and the equipment that many changed over to the legal way and made it on a larger scale. The first licensed distillery was opened by George Smith – farmer, architect, scholar, illicit whisky distiller and smuggler. He made a whisky reputed to be 'great'.

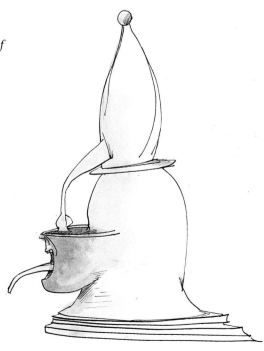

Glen GARIOCH Moofling and the ANGEL'S SHARE.

PEATREEK SPIRITS – GLEN GARIOCH

In the dying glow of eventide it is quite possible to see the Mungling Peaty Sploons swirling away above the pagodas' darkened arrowheads, towards the angels' heavenly cloisters, as the new barley is smoked to perfection. The angels wait, sniff the air and, in the fullness of a man's mortal time, swoop down and euphungulate above the place where man stores his liquid treasure securely and secretly as though it were his and his alone. The angels have an eternity to drink their fill whenever they wish, and hover in eternal contemplation. Every distillery has about it and above itself a brooding stealth like this, which can only be the result of intense accounting and continuous assessment, the gatherings of peatreek accumulations in dark corners and the eventual balance of the final product. No angel will take more than its share, nor would a Scotsman allow it. These are the avowed facts of life and the tragic sadness in a Scotsman's soul is because of them. Even 1% of his issue is too much (if it hasnae bin paid fur), though every Scotsman will agree that the making of it is as free as the water and the earth from which it springs. It pours merrily by the gallon, 24 hours a day, into the locked implacability of a spirit safe, beyond the man's reach to drink of, as he may. And yet there, above his very head, in the air of Scotland's freedom, 190 million gallons of tantalising vapours escape each year and hang there, mocking the anger of every customs man. That is the Scotsman's frustration and his sweet revenge.

A SCOTTISH ANGEL WAITING FOR HIS 20%

IAN MACDONALD I.S.O., *late of the Inland Revenue and author of a classic work on whisky,* Smuggling in The Highlands (1914), *was a severe late-Victorian excise man who wielded a rod of iron in high moral dudgeon across the vast regions north of Inverness. He considered the virulent revival of illicit distilling to strike at the very fibre of social stability, quoting as causes the abolition of the Malt Tax, the diminished powers of the Revenue Preventative Staff and the Crofters Act of 1886. The latter gave the descendants of the dispossessed crofters their land back, and their houses,* most of which had been built by the crofters themselves. This new security of tenure engendered a vigorous confidence in some kind of future and revived those pernicious habits of bygone days. A young generation returned to the old traditions and skills. Peatreek was rampant again. *Officer* IAN MACDONALD *wrote: 'In their efforts to suppress this fresh outbreak the Revenue officials were much hampered not only by the strong popular sentiment in favour of smuggling and smugglers, but also by the mistaken leniency of local magistrates, and by the weak, temporising policy of the Board of* Inland Revenue towards certain sportsmen who claimed exemption for their extensive deer forests from visits by the Inland Revenue officials.'

There was never any doubt when OFFICER HOSIE
SPITTLE OF GLENSHEE was back in the TAY Valley region
of his boyhood years, for he never passed through Aberfeldy
without buying a fresh supply of tweeds from Haggarts, the
milliners of that very town. This sartorial snooper would
make his discreet enquiries there during his intimate fitting-
room struggles, and at Fanny Dullweem's Cake Bazaar
afterwards where he bought his toffees and oatcakes to see
him through another fruitless night of surveillance. He
never gave up hope of catching sight of the telltale peatsmoke
whispers rising above poplars and rowan trees along the
river banks before sundown. He came every autumn as the
leaves turned to rich orange hues, stabbing the black green
conifers like bothy fires. It gladdened his heart. Many times
he would swoop but every time he was fooled. Leaf burning
would be in full swing and smoke was in the air like
Scottish gossip. He only ever caught old Mr Haggart himself,
behind the very shop burning some tweed offcuts from last
year's range, the same as this year's but last year's
nevertheless. Officer Hosie bought three more suits by way of
apology.

Stylish to the point of lunacy, CYRUS CULBOKIE from the
BLACK ISLE, NORTH OF INVERNESS who was nicknamed
the 'Wretched White Watch' on account of his cloak of white
menace that could be seen from 20 miles off. Although he
crawled on his stomach whilst stalking his prey, his
ridiculous purple heather feather plume strutted above him
as conspicuously as a pipe band of Sutherland Highlanders.
He took up pipe smoking after the manner of a popular new
detective hero he had tried to read. He eventually earned the
title of the 'Wretched Burn Watch' when he accidentally set
fire to a thousand square miles of prime grouse moor heather
whilst trying to light his pipe in a high wind.

TAMDHU Railway STATION Distillery SHOP and TOURIST ATTRACTION

Aberfeldy

Ralph Steadman

Aberfeldy distillery was established in 1898, on the road to Perth, on the south side of the River Tay. Fresh spring water is taken from the nearby Pitilie Burn to produce this unique single malt with its distinctive peaty nose, its rasping good looks, energy-saving panty hose . . . what? And 43% volume beyond the thighs of the most prodigious siren and only 15 years old – goddammit! What a whisky!! – and it's got a kind of squirrel on it. Very light, not unlike Caol Ila, a similar kind of label, and a similar kind of squirrel. The classic kind to instil confidence and an expensive response

ABERFELDY Distillery — PERTHSHIRE

from a potential customer. It was at this point that I realised that all distilleries have managers. It took me back to the time when I was working in Woolworths as a trainee manager, and I found myself struggling on the floor of the stockroom with the manager himself, who did not like me, or that is the impression I got, for we were locked in mortal combat amongst collapsing storage shelves. It was at that point that I was asked to leave. I finished making the refuse paper bail I had started, dusted myself off, left as quietly as I dared, and started all over again.

BUGS in the BARLEY. KNOW YOUR ENEMY

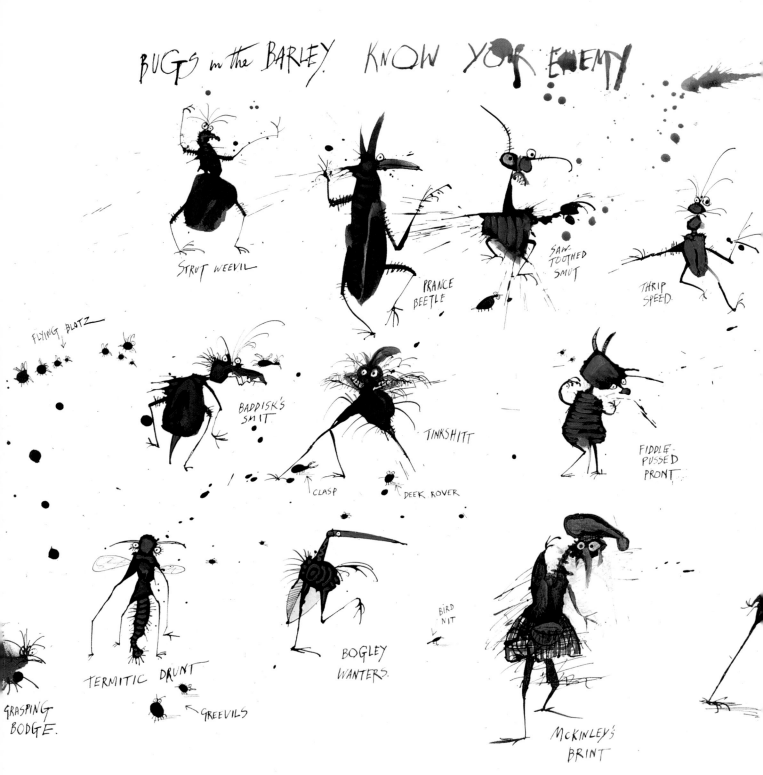

STRUT WEEVIL

PRANCE BEETLE

SAW-TOOTHED SMUT

THRIP SPEED.

FLYING BLOTZ

BADDISK'S SMIT.

TINKSHITT

FIDDLE-PUSSED PRONT.

CLASP

DEEK ROVER

TERMITIC DRUNT

BOGLEY WANTERS.

BIRD NIT

GRASPING BODGE.

GREEVILS

McKINLEY'S BRINT

Grain, i.e. rye, wheat, corn and barley, is very wholesome, loved by rats and other vermin the world over and there is plenty of it. Great pyramids of the stuff lie in dry temperate conditions all over Scotland, and in sweating, corrugated store shacks, secret hideouts far away from the people it was originally intended for, in Third World countries.

Grain provides a gluttonous beggars' banquet of monumental proportions for strange and irksome pests. Silophilos Granarias, Rhyzopentha Dominica, Staphylinidae or Cryptophagus, if you can pronounce them, are the little swines among others, that meld with this abundance and creepy crawly their way through pyramids of stored grain like Brits on

DOGGLE LICE

CRINGE GRAIN

-URGLE-SHUNT

LONG-NECKED PREEN

GODGER'S LUDDITE

round dish which shakes them rigid from where they are tossed into an experiment tray and wish they had never been born. By this time you are itching all over just watching them and you feel no pity; just an uncontrollable desire to get away and take a shower.

Grain is described in various ways. It is referred to as 'bleached' barley when treated with sulphur. If it is naturally good in colour and, untreated, it is known as 'bright' barley. If blight is present in the kernels or mould is settling, then it is called 'blighted'. If smutty spores appear on a mound of stored barley, then they have a word for that too – they call it 'smutty'.

Barley can be 'ergoty', where garlic cloves have accidentally got mixed with the batch, though this only happens when someone is desperately trying to disguise the smell of whisky on the breath. But, the real menace is the weevil, and they have a word for that too – yes! – 'weevily'.

These are, of course, very scientific descriptions and the layman would be wise to let the experts bandy these various condition descriptions about. Otherwise confusion will result.

Generally, the layman will be best advised, when being given a ton of grain to lift, to exclaim: 'Wow! This batch of grain sure is infected. Smell those smut balls!' Though don't play this trick too often because these conditions are rare. Grain experts are fastidiously vigilant and can spot a weevil at 20 paces in a 15 ton pile – and ZAP! They detect an undesirable odour characteristic long before you do – and it could quite as easily be you they smell, thus provoking an embarrassing incident. Don't be a smart arse. Let the expert tell you. Not many people show a big interest in creepy crawlies so if you do, listen and learn; then when you get home you will be able to identify the ones you find in your porridge and muesli packets. The kids can learn a lot that way too.

PARASITE

PAPER TURGE LICE

holiday. It is a sharp eye you need to notice a moving grain, since their camouflage is almost perfect. If they are being watched they stop and play dead. Just whistle to yourself and pretend not to notice, as you sidle over with a grain snatch to scoop up the filthy little beggars before they burrow back inside the pile. Then you pour them into a vibrating merry-go-

Morrison's Glen Garioch Distillery, Old Meldrum, Aberdeenshire

Glen Garioch

Old Meldrum is the village attached to and developed around the distillery known as Glen Garioch. It has a quaint air of old worldliness about it and a terrible chip shop. The distillery is particularly interesting in that the heat generated during the distilling process is not wasted but piped through a huge greenhouse complex throughout the year. Tomato plants are trained horizontally along tracks supported by intermittent strings. This enables the plants to grow many yards away from their richly fed rooting system to sustain anything up to 60 bunches of tomatoes per plant. A truly Scottish characteristic in action.

The manager is a warm and hospitable man who allowed my nephew and his crew to film whatever they may. They had come to see me on the job and film me in action.

Unfortunately they had left by the time Ian Fyfe decided to break into song (see page 6).

We tried the 10, 15 and 21 year-old single malts. Sublime unctions culminating in the softer 21 year-old. The 15 year-old hid the heart of an athlete and was at optimum state for drinking. Age too can blunt the true nature of a single malt.

Glen Garioch – Founded 1797 by Ingram Lamb and Co. 1840, bought by John Manson then J.F. Thompson of Leith. 2 maltings – barley was grown in the neighbourhood. Peat kiln. Mash tun 14 feet diameter. Wort in underback – 3,000 gallons. 3 washbacks – 5,000 gallons. Wash charger of oak to serve the stills. Wash still 1,900 gallons. Worm tub 40 feet long and 5 feet deep. Low wines still – 1,500 gallons. 12 men employed. Local peat. Water from Fircock Hill. 50,000 gallons per year.

Longmorn Distillery

Fettercairn DISTILLERY KINCARDINE Highlands EAST and BOSWELL the ABERDEEN ANGUS — Ralph Steadman

Fettercairn

Traditionally it never needed many to make it – one to distil and one to look out for the gauger . . .

It is one of the oldest distilleries and went legal in 1824. Its water comes from high up in the Cairngorms and it is situated on flat lands, near the North Esk river. It is now very high-tech and, true to its tradition, requires practically no one to run it.

The stories are legion about how people escape with spirit from distilleries. The long thin tube in the trousers, for example, or the guy who brought a bottle of milk in with him every day. He always went home with the bottle full, never drank it. Actually it was filled with whisky when he went home, but you would never know, because it was painted white on the inside.

Anonymous

A delicious, fine, strong, rippling muscularity defines this most famous of single malts for me. Sometimes, I start thinking that it is over-praised, yet, grudgingly, I have to acknowledge its pedigree. It is one of Scotland's flagship exports and has enjoyed the best of everything for so long that I often resist buying it, since it does all right without my patronage. However, when I do buy a bottle, it always lives beyond the opinion that settles upon me like misty rain, and I have to admit how fine it really is.

"The GLENLIVET" Distillery, Ballindalloch, Ba

...hire (SPEYSIDE)   Ralph STEADman

Frank A. Perret, an American volcanologist, listens to his patent seismic microphone in the early pre-prohibition days. He was able to detect the subterranean rumblings and analyse the pitch of the sounds and, thus, calculate the time of an eruption. Bootleggers seized on the idea as a bogus scientific front for an illicit still, standing about for hours listening to the sounds of the bubbling wash and declaring an imminent eruption of pure hooch on the market.

FRANK A. PERRET an American Volcanologist listens to his patent SEISMIC MICROPHONE in the early PRE-PROHIBITION days. He was able to detect the Subterranean rumblings and analyse the pitch of the sounds and thus calculate the time of an eruption. BOOTLEGGERS seized on the idea as a bogus scientific front for an illicit still, standing about for hours listening to the sounds of a bubbling WASH + 'declaring' an imminent eruption of 'PURE HOOCH on the MARKET.

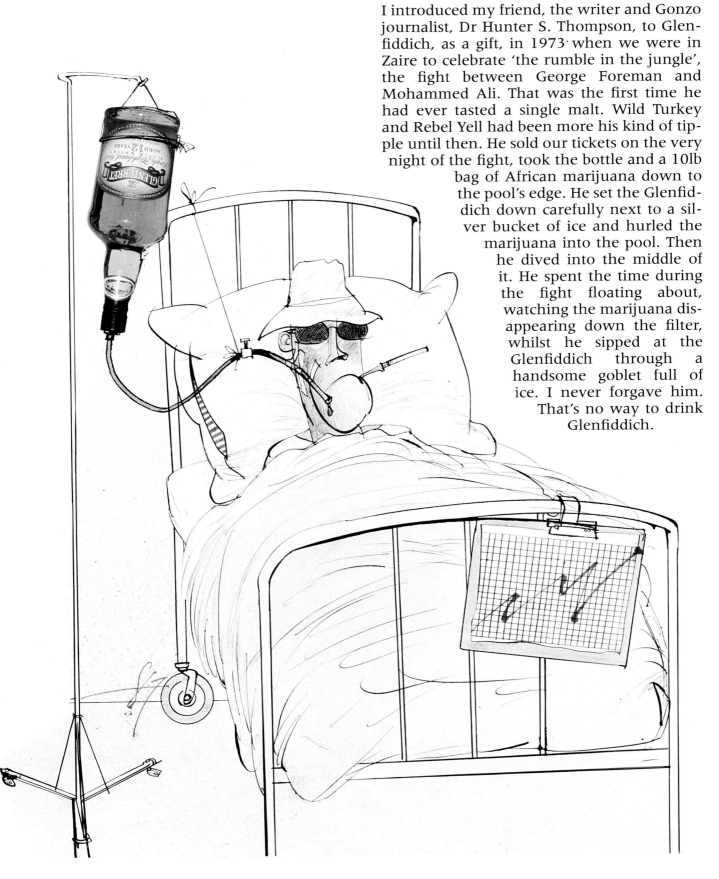

I introduced my friend, the writer and Gonzo journalist, Dr Hunter S. Thompson, to Glenfiddich, as a gift, in 1973 when we were in Zaire to celebrate 'the rumble in the jungle', the fight between George Foreman and Mohammed Ali. That was the first time he had ever tasted a single malt. Wild Turkey and Rebel Yell had been more his kind of tipple until then. He sold our tickets on the very night of the fight, took the bottle and a 10lb bag of African marijuana down to the pool's edge. He set the Glenfiddich down carefully next to a silver bucket of ice and hurled the marijuana into the pool. Then he dived into the middle of it. He spent the time during the fight floating about, watching the marijuana disappearing down the filter, whilst he sipped at the Glenfiddich through a handsome goblet full of ice. I never forgave him. That's no way to drink Glenfiddich.

GEORGE DICKEL WAS A PERFECTIONIST WITH A VISION—YESSIR! IN THE SWEEPIN' VALLEYS OF TENNESSEE GRAIN GROWIN' COUNTRY, THE SWEET TASTIN' LIMESTONE WATERS CAME A-CASCADIN' DOWN FROM THEM HILLS AND A-COOLIN' THE HOT-HEADED DREAM OF OLE GEORGE DICKEL HIMSEL'... WHY, I'VE HEARD TELL THAT WITH ONE ~~SINGLE~~ HAND BEHIND HIS BACK AN' ONE FOOT IN CASCADE HOLLOW, OLE GEORGE COULD STILL MAKE THE FINEST SMOOTHEST SIPPIN' WHISKY IN THE WORLD—YESSIR!

Bunnahabhain Distillery - Islay.   Ralph Steadman

Ralph STEADman   Crofts, Islay 3 Sept 91

SKEYBURN ROTHES   RALSTEAD

Tasting single malts is surely an impeccable art of the highest calibre, but testing yourself to destruction is surely the highest art, and perhaps the very lowest. What kind of hang-over is peculiar to each delectable malt and to each person? Everybody has a story to tell. It affects everybody differently. How can you be an expert if you haven't blasted a hole in the side of every one of over 200 sin-gle malts in existence? A sip is merely a whiff of promise. It hardly represents the full experience that every expert claims to have. No, you need to be face down with one cheek in the gutter and the other hard against the pavement, the empty bottle by your side and the disgust of every passerby thumping down on you like loose rocks on a mountain pass in the rain. You need to feel so goddamn wretched that you never want to drink again, not at least for 24 hours any-way. The fact is, if you feel like this, you have not been drinking single malts at all, but one or other of those rotten blends that hit the market from time to time, like cheap toy reproductions of a London bus, assum-ing authentic souvenir status, or empty hot

chestnuts from a street vendor's brazier in Oxford Street.

During one of my sojourns north, in search of the 'full experience', I was accused of destroying one full bottle of 12 year-old Highland Park from a first-fill oloroso sherry cask at 96.6 degrees proof. It was a hideous personal attack by an acknowledged bard and eloquent critic of all things malted, a member of The Scotch Malt Whisky Associ-ation, for which he is treasurer, taster, adviser, sage, Druid, poet, on-the spot-reporter and raconteur. He is Anthony Troon. The scene was the Kirkwall Hotel in the Orkneys. The hotel bar. I was amongst friends, and he was welcome, so much so that he saw fit to disappear and re-appear 5 minutes later with the aforesaid Highland Park 12 year-old. I was confronted with what amounted to 'a serious tasting'. You cannot muck about with these things. You have to engage in full frontal attack. This I did, with the collusion, and I might add, encouragement, of my companions who included John Hughes, the Famous Grouse-man of Matthew Gloag & Son, Ltd, aided

and abetted by Gordon Kerr, marketing man and creative drink-inducer of Messrs Odd-bins Ltd, tireless purveyors of liquid refreshment nationwide. What was I to do? My wife Anna was there. I was safe, and she is no lover of whisky. Her share was mine. The bottle was plied like a tyre lever, plunged into the glass and then swiftly seesawed upwards to be slammed down on the table as if it were an alcoholic steam hammer. The bottle was soon empty, or so it seemed. I don't recall exactly, though later I was systematically accused of being the bottle's destroyer in Anthony Troon's lyrical column in *The Scotsman*. This could not be true, however, since the very day after the tasting I felt absolutely fine and as interested in my surroundings as any roving reporter of my genre.

I can only assume that the purest single malts of the finest pedigree leave no harmful poisons behind to be dealt with later by the various useful organs of the body.

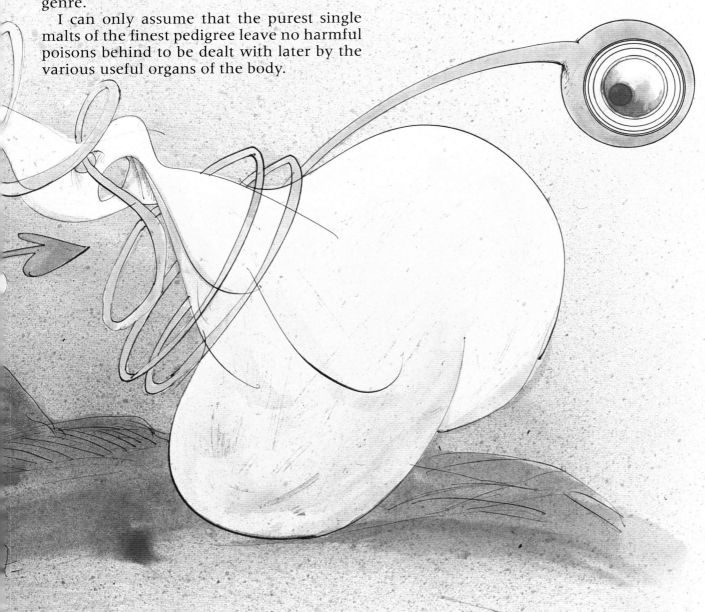

There is a place called Ferintosh on the Black Isle near Dingwall, which has been the hotbed of illicit distilling for longer than anyone knows and an 'Ancient Brewery of Antiquity' to boot. 'More whisky was distilled here than in all the rest of Scotland', it is claimed. It was land acquired by the 5th Laird of Culloden, Duncan Forbes, a loyal Hanoverian, from the Mackintosh of Mackintosh in 1626.

The Jacobites slashed and burned 1,800 acres of his farmland for his allegiance, yet allowed him to distil and sell duty-free whisky in exchange for 400 Merks (Scottish coin of the period attached firmly to a long chain) plus some whisky. His family made a fortune over the next 100 years, undercutting everyone in sight and running at least 6 distilleries. The privilege was curtailed during the lifetime of

Burns, who wrote a sad ode in memory. Beón Wyvis, the name of a mountain towering above Dingwall, gave its name to a major new distillery built on the site in 1879, close to Cromarty Firth but not close enough. A pipeline had to be brought from Loch Ussie, three and a half miles away, according to Alfred Barnard, the 19th-century chronicler of distilleries. It was into Loch Ussie that the Highland mystic Brahan Seer threw his Stone of Vision and his silver kilt when sentenced to death for the heretical prophecy that Scotland would go legal by 1823. Taking a deep breath, he called out to the depths, 'Ya has nae need for a stone o' Vayen nae a silver kilt wi' no peatreek in Hell!' No one quite knew what he meant, so his words were passed on down the generations as Scottish wisdom.

INDEX